Pre-Grouping Trains on
BRITISH RAILWAYS

The LNER Companies

Frontispiece: Exuding power, but with ample grace, an A8 4-6-2 tank stands at York Station. These locomotives were an LNER rebuild of the final North Eastern tank design, which was to the rarely used 4-4-4 wheel arrangement.

Pre-Grouping Trains on BRITISH RAILWAYS

The LNER Companies

Peter Hay

Oxford Publishing Co.

Dedication

For A.H.G.
my mentor in North Britain

ISBN 0 86093 315 6

A FOULIS-OPC Railway Book

© 1984 P. Hay & Oxford Publishing Co.
Reprinted 1988

British Library Cataloguing in Publication Data

Hay, Peter, *1932—*
    Pre-grouping trains on British Railways—
    The LNER companies.
    1. London and North Eastern Railway—History—
    Pictorial works
    2. Locomotives—Great Britain—History—
    Pictorial works
    I. Title
    625.2'61'0941   TJ603.4.G72L66

Published by:
Haynes Publishing Group
Sparkford, Near Yeovil, Somerset. BA22 7JJ

Haynes Publications Inc.
861 Lawrence Drive, Newbury Park, California 91320, USA.

Contents

Preface

This book is one of the results of a misspent youth, and is also a record of survivals. To many people interested in railways, anything from the pre-grouping companies has a special quality, at least partly derived from their great individuality. This fascination holds enthusiasts who never knew the old companies and perhaps even people who were not born when these pictures were taken although, I suspect, they feel that things produced by the 'Big Four' also have the same special attraction. Their relics certainly disappeared faster from the railway scene, a loss that was largely due to the wholesale changes in traction and rolling stock, to say nothing of line closures.

The regions which were previously part of the LNER changed as much and as quickly as any others, but it was not always so. From 1923 to 1950 the company and its successor seemed to have made less progress in replacing old with new equipment than in other parts of the country. This was mainly because a great deal of revenue in the area had traditionally come from heavy industries like coal and steel and, when these industries nearly collapsed in the disastrous trade slump between the wars, the railway's profitability disappeared. No doubt this enforced policy of make-do-and-mend sorely tried those who had to run the railway, but it provided for years a happy hunting ground for those in search of relics from the past. The further away from London the more there was to be seen, and even express engines from before 1923 were still running. The Great Northern Railway was the exception as the Ponies and Atlantics had all gone by 1951, although the Class A3

Pacifics had GNR origins. In England, 4-4-0 locomotives of Great Central, Great Eastern and North Eastern build were still active while the GER 'Claud Hamilton' class was very numerous indeed once one was beyond somewhere like Cambridge, having its fair share of named trains to work, especially in the summer. Much of East Anglia seemed to have changed little between the wars, and this feeling of time gone by was strong on the railway too, whether it was the rusticity of the Aldeburgh branch or a 'Claud Hamilton' class locomotive bustling along with a light train.

Further north, the Cheshire Lines services were often worked by GCR 'Director' class engines, while GCR goods locomotives were common over a very wide area. In North Yorkshire and County Durham, once away from the East Coast Main Line, the atmosphere was very strongly North Eastern including several rope-worked inclines of great age. The mineral traffic, although greatly reduced from its heyday, was operated almost entirely by North Eastern engines, often hauling their distinctive high-sided coal wagons. In Scotland, too, there were express engines at work to be photographed, as well as many other relics from a glorious and, in one case, inglorious past.

Of pre-grouping carriages and wagons, there was still a good variety to be seen and here the GNR contributed its share, although Gresley's continuous responsibility for carriages and wagons since 1905 may have had something to do with it. I have not tried to distinguish his pre and post-grouping carriage designs where they appear in these pictures, as such discrimination is for the experts. My regret

Plate 1: A complete pre-grouping ensemble of wooden trestle, Class F5 No. 67189 (GER Class M15) and three GER coaches. The scene is on the branch from Witham to Maldon in Essex, photographed in 1956.

is that I didn't take nearly as many pictures of old carriages as I could have done, engines being the main attraction. For this reason, the pre-grouping carriages all too often appear in this book as appendages to the principal subject of the picture, but I have tried to point them out where they do appear, with as much accuracy as I can manage. Part of the problem of identification comes from the fact that while books on engine history are common, carriage history is only just being written about in similar detail. Perhaps one should not be too critical about this lack of material, seeing that some companies have only had their annals written in superficial outline, and still await the kind of thorough treatment which George Dow has given the GCR.

Each of the six companies which amalgamated to form the LNER has a section to itself, and the objects in the pictures were those which were on that line, although some of them came from other constituent companies. In the text which introduces each section I have tried to do two things, the first of which is to give some idea of the general impression I got — the feel of the place — when visiting the lines and area of each company. This is bound to be selective, because I was not able to go everywhere but, at the same time, subjective. No doubt any other visitor would have taken away quite a different impression, and I am sure that enthusiasts who have grown up in the area concerned, would have yet another view of what things were like.

The other thing I have tried to do in the text is to treat it as a record of visits made and tours undertaken, so the sequence of pictures roughly follows my journeys around each area. There were, in the 1950s, so many places to seek out in pursuit of the pre-grouping scene that even centres offering great riches, like Hull, rarely got a second visit. When I did arrive at a particular section of the network, my wanderings were rarely guided by local knowledge because so often they were just trips of discovery, in what the grapevine whispered were promising places. Therefore these pictures are one man's view, but perhaps they have some interest for being unguided, as here you see the everyday and sometimes, very rarely, and then often by chance, what was unusual at that place and time.

In writing the captions I have made my own rules, for better or worse. The subject is identified by class as well as number, and here I have generally used the LNER classification with occasional reference to the pre-grouping one. I think every location is identified, sometimes with an indication of how other lines in the picture fit into the local geography, and occasionally I was sufficiently wide awake to record exactly which train was photographed. Perhaps those who love timetables may get some pleasure from looking up the train I mention but be warned; my memory, like yours, is fallible, and if you have records they are almost certainly more to be relied on. The same goes for my identification of the ancestry of carriages.

This is the point at which to record my debt to those who have collected and published information about the old companies and their doings. I must give special mention to those unsung heroes of the Railway Correspondence & Travel Society, whose monumental series on locomotive history gives both a delightful vista and a positive quarry of facts. My own contribution to it is imperceptible, but my debt is great.

Altogether the LNER area was indeed rewarding to the photographer trying to record the scene and its objects before scrapping and modernisation. The Beeching axe caused it to vanish forever. To those of my readers who never saw it, my condolences, and let us hope this book doesn't make you envious; I wish you had been there. To those who were, I hope it brings back some of your memories.

Plate 2: The Chesham branch train on its way to Chalfont, behind a GCR Class C13 4-4-2 tank, in June 1958. The coaches originated as a District Railway electric train in 1899.

Plate 3: The North Eastern Railway's improvements to its main line included the provision of through roads for non-stopping trains at several of the principal stations on the East Coast route. Selby compromised this assistance to fast running by a heavy speed restriction over the swingbridge north of the station. Class B16 No. 61450, (NER Class S3) very much in original form, accelerates an express goods southwards on 28th August 1952.

Of the LNER constituents, only the Great Eastern Railway had a nickname, 'The Sweedie'. Did it have its origins on the Stock Exchange? Certainly brokers and their clients would rarely have blessed their investment, for returns on GER stock were always modest. Frugal but reliable might have been a good description, once the horrors of receivership in the 1860s were left behind. The slender prosperity was earned in hard times, for the great agricultural depression, which started in the 1870s, sorely tried the farmers of those wide-horizoned acres. Yet the Great Eastern Railway steadily multiplied its lines and, in the end, there were few corners of Essex, Suffolk, or Norfolk which had none of its stations. Few other companies cast envious eyes over GER territory, and the interpenetrating tangles of the coalfield area were unknown. Only the Great Northern Railway to the west offered any competition for the farmers' traffic, although the Midland Railway's bold stroke of snapping up the London, Tilbury & Southend Railway was typical of Derby's imperialism. So too was their incursion by the creation of the Midland & Great Northern Joint Railway out of the ramshackle local enterprises of North Norfolk.

I don't know if the LNER benefited much from the resurgence in agriculture in the 1930s, although it may have saved some lines which otherwise would have perished. The slaughter, when it came in the 1950s and 1960s, was desperate, but the GER's creation of its network before the turn of the century had been economically done. 'The Sweedie' was a line that gave the impression, to use an old saying, of 'making half a crown do the work of five bob' and, as a result, we could rejoice in some notable survivals. The last examples of that Victorian workhorse, the 2-4-0 tender engine, were found on the GER, and the carriages seemed to linger on too. An examination of the locomotive withdrawal lists of the late 1950s reveals some surprising companions in the scrapyards, with no less than four distinct generations of East Anglian passenger engines being withdrawn at the same time. These were the Class E4 2-4-0 locomotives, the 'Claud Hamilton' class, which succeeded the Class E4s, the Class B12 4-6-0s which succeeded in their turn, and Gresley's 'Sandringham' class, which took over the best trains from the Class B12s. With the goods traffic it was the same, as engines of the 19th and 20th centuries went to the scrapyards side by side, with Class J15, J17, J19 and J39 engines working and vanishing together. Stratford, which held the world speed record for locomotive construction (a Class J15 locomotive in 9¾ hours in 1891) built soundly as well as speedily.

My introduction to the Great Eastern Railway was at Liverpool Street, in those grim years immediately after the war. I will never forget my first visit there because as the Westinghouse pumps panted and thumped, a vision appeared amid the smoke and grime. It was one of the first of Thompson's Class B1 locomotives, resplendent in apple green. Not only did the colour positively glow among the dirty black engines which surrounded it, but there was polished brass to go with the green and, the greatest wonder of all, a white cab roof. I had never seen anything like it before in my life. On subsequent visits I found my way to Stratford, and discovered the delights of alternative routes. Rightly or wrongly, an Underground ticket from Victoria to Stratford was acceptable by tube the whole way, or by steam from Liverpool Street. Even more useful than this was the fact that one could return on a steam train by way of Fenchurch Street, over the little-used spur to Bow Junction. That was an experience too, as I had never travelled in

coaches where the partitions between the compartments only went to shoulder height. Climbing along the coach from compartment to compartment was a real novelty, although the occasional passenger on whose head we descended didn't think so.

Stratford was not only an introduction to a wider range of GER engines and trains, but it also gave an acquaintance with the North Woolwich branch passing underneath, on which the engines with passenger trains seemed to be mainly 2-4-2 tanks. One murky and memorable afternoon, when I was admiring one of Mr Holden's Class F5 engines at North Woolwich, I was told by the driver, in all seriousness, that 'if you want to see the big engines you'll have to go up to London', advice which I heeded. In the 1950s, the 'three generations of engines' phenomenon could be seen on the branch with 'Buck Jumpers' (Class J67), 'Gobblers' (Classes F5 and F6) and Class N7 tanks, all taking a turn with the workings.

My first experience of the GER outside London took me to Cambridge, and that was a revelation. In retrospect, nearly every train seems to have been worked by a pre-grouping engine, although it can't really have been so, even on a summer Saturday, but the impression which remains is of a steady procession of trains headed by one 'Claud Hamilton' after another. The icing on the cake was the first sight of a Class E4 2-4-0, a design of venerable ancestry and virtually extinct elsewhere. They worked the Mildenhall branch trains from the north end of the lengthy Cambridge platform, and through the Colne Valley to Colchester from the other end. As well as a feast of old engines, quite a lot of the main line and branch line trains contained Great Eastern Railway coaches. Of the Cambridge of the Backs and King's College Chapel I saw nothing, nor have I to this day. The station with its marvels has always been the attraction.

Throughout the rest of the 1950s 'The Sweedie' maintained its identity strongly in East Anglia as a whole, and even in the London area, where its engines were still to be seen. Admittedly the Chingford, the North Woolwich, the Ongar and other suburban branches eventually lost their GER flavour, but one did not have to go far into the country to find active pre-grouping relics. Most memorable was a grand photographic tour, moving in a wide sweep round from Ongar, taking in Huntingdonshire, the Isle of Ely and North Norfolk before reaching the coast at Lowestoft and coming back by way of Aldeburgh and the Witham branches, to Maldon and Braintree. The great Norfolk & Suffolk Joint line swingbridge across Breydon Water was still in place, and so was Aldeburgh's ancient all-over roof. The branch driver there was reputed to be a perfectionist, and it was said that his 2-4-2 tank was as carefully prepared for its eight mile trip to Saxmundham and back as it would have been for working an Edinburgh non-stop. Great Eastern engines also worked much of the Midland & Great Northern Joint Railway system, though my acquaintance with that highly individual concern was not extensive.

The outline of most of the GER engines pictured here had not been greatly changed since the Grouping, but the two large passenger classes were an exception. Both the 'Claud Hamilton' class and the Class B12 locomotives had been given new round-topped boilers by the LNER, which happily ensured their survival, but the Class B12s which had been sent to the Great North of Scotland system were an exception. Many of them retained a truly pre-grouping outline, with Belpaire boilers and GER style chimneys, although, unlike some of the 'Claud Hamilton' engines.

they had all lost their slotted valances. Scotland even managed to get some of them into the apple green livery although, elsewhere, former GER engines were black, often unlined, and sometimes none too clean. The smaller country sheds often managed to do better, and there are happy memories of polished brass beading round the splashers of someone's favourite 'Claud Hamilton'. The pre-grouping silhouettes of the smaller engines were very distinctive, 'with an unusual habit of siting the dome well forward, close up behind the chimney, with safety-valves occupying the middle of the boiler and remote from the cab windows. The 1950s saw the demise of most of the GER classes, being succeeded in the end by electric trains and diesel locomotives.

East Anglia was well served by the GER in its day, and the LNER after it. For some people that part of our country is a view of lonely churches, deserted under enormous skies but, for me, the scene also contains a Class J15 quietly pottering along with a few wagons on an afternoon goods train, or a 'Claud Hamilton' and three coaches making a leisurely wayside call at a station on one of those long straggling branches. It is a sunny day, but a keen wind coming straight across the open country whips the smoke and steam horizontally away from the engine. It is also a long way away from the smokey cavern of Liverpool Street, and the hectic suburban rush hours. With both kinds of country to serve, from which to try to make a profit, 'The Sweedie' didn't have an easy time of it, but made a brave show. We were grateful for its personality, and for its survival.

Plate 4: An attraction at Cambridge was the Mildenhall branch train, often worked by a Class E4 2-4-0 tender engine. In this view, No. 62796 pulls away from the main line at Barnwell Junction with an afternoon train in April 1956. Barnwell Station is on the branch and just out of sight to the left. Virtually every piece of railway equipment in this picture, except the main line track, is GER.

Plate 5: In June 1958 Liverpool Street's smokey gloom makes a fitting background for one of the last batch of GER type suburban tanks. Class N7 No. 69725 was, in fact, built by the LNER in 1928.

Plate 6: In contrast to its grimy counterparts, No. 68619 was selected for special livery and cleaning as showpiece pilot at Liverpool Street. In February 1957, however, it was keeping strange company at New Cross Gate, on the Southern Region, reached by way of the East London line. Standard 2-6-4 tank No. 80032 is alongside.

Plate 7: The electrification which drove out the suburban tanks was much in evidence on the main line at Stratford, in June 1954, when Class B12 No. 61557 (GER Class 1500) had charge of the steam crane which was needed on the Southend line. The old coaches are Great Northern Railway stock.

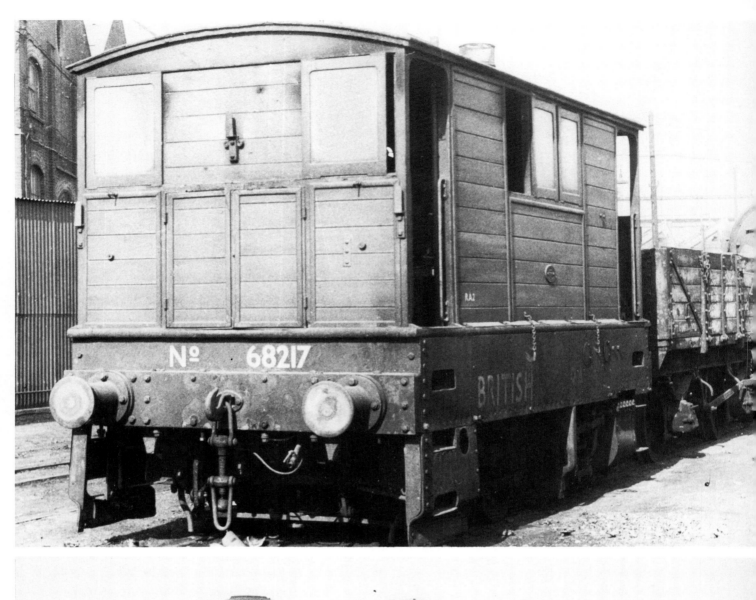

Plate 8 (left upper): Any visit to Stratford Shed would produce something of interest to a photographer. This 0-6-0 tram engine was built as a member of GER Class C53 to work the Wisbech & Upwell Tramway in 1903, and was awaiting scrapping some fifty years later.

Plate 9 (left lower): The powerful 0-4-0 tanks of Class Y4 were built in 1913 as GER Class B74, and were mainly used to shunt some of the awkward corners at Mile End. The safety valves are buried in coal, and presumably the driver looked out round the side. Note the dumb buffers for the sharp curves, the iron toolbox on the footplating, and the peculiar rear guard irons. The chimney is of the final GER parallel-sided pattern.

Plate 10 (above): The distinctive skyline of a Class J67 tank at Stratford in 1953. Putting the dome well forward was a Holden trademark. As can be imagined, the short wheelbase gave a lively ride at speed, and may have given rise to the nickname 'Buck Jumpers' by which this class was known. Behind the engine we can see the enormous stacks of locomotive coal, walled in with larger lumps. In the distance are the signals for one of Stratford's many junctions.

Plate 11 (below): The low level lines at Stratford produced much variety in engines, but Class J69 No. 68579, although built for passenger work in 1896, was something of a rarity on such duties 60 years later. The scene is near Stratford Market Station, and the train is bound for North Woolwich. This picture provides a good view of the Gresley-designed quintuple articulated sets, introduced circa 1925.

Plate 13 (right upper):   Class F5 (GER Class M15) No. 67211 was one of the earlier Great Eastern 2-4-2 tanks, with a plain cab, and is pictured still with its condensing gear for use on the East London line. The headcode indicates a North Woolwich to Palace Gates train. The 'quint-art' sets had a brake van at one end only, so the guard could sometimes be at the front of the train, next to the engine, as is the case here.

Plate 14 (right lower):   Branching off the Cambridge main line at Audley End was a connection to Bartlow on the Haverhill line, although by 1952 most trains went no further than the first station, Saffron Walden. No. 67322, (NER Class O), a G5 0-4-4 tank, was the branch engine, and the push-pull set is of GER origin. The leading coach has the high roof and vertical panelling, which was adopted in 1906, while the other coach is older, being one of the GER's first bogie designs, of 1897. It offered first and third class compartments, a lavatory and a luggage compartment, all in a body length of under 50ft.

Plate 12 (above):   South of Stratford, the lines to North Woolwich made numerous connections with the Port of London Authority lines serving London docks, and once carried a very substantial goods traffic. For this reason an extra pair of running lines was provided, seen on the right in this picture. Class F6 No. 67228 (GER Class G69) carries a version of the 1920 GER disc headcode, and has the large windowed cab.

Plate 15: Nearer Cambridge at Shelford, the line from Bartlow and points east, including the Colne Valley, joins the main line. Class J15 No. 6545 (GER Class Y14) heads a three coach train of GER stock from Cambridge to Colchester in the summer of 1956.

Plate 16: The principal attraction at Cambridge was the profusion of Class D16 'Claud Hamilton' engines. All the survivors had the large round-topped boiler but some, like No. 62605, retained the decorative valances over the coupling rods. The scene is just north of Cambridge, at Coldham Lane Junction where the Newmarket line came in. The main line has been relaid with BR flat-bottomed rail, but the branch retains its LNER bullhead track.

Plate 17:   Class D16 (GER Class H88) No. **62564** is at the head of the 4.05p.m. Cambridge to March, via St. Ives, train in April 1956. Across the Cam River Bridge was the signal box controlling the junction for the St. Ives line, the third and northernmost of the junctions on the main line immediately north of Cambridge, the other two being at Coldham Lane *(Plate 16)* and Barnwell *(Plate 4)*.

Plate 18:   Two steam veterans, in a photograph taken near Cambridge. On the right is No. **62530** with a fast train from Ely, while on the left is a two cylinder compound traction engine. In the 1950s, both of these could have been bought for virtually their scrap metal value, a saddening thought. The yard beside the line was crowded with traction engines waiting to be cut up for scrap.

Plate 19 (right upper): Class D16 No. 62571 has a clear road at Cherry Hinton Crossing, on the Cambridge to Newmarket line. Great Eastern Railway signals like this one, on its tall wooden post, were often visible for great distances across the Fens.

Plate 20 (right lower): Mildenhall trains crossed the Ely to Newmarket line at Fordham Junction, where we see this early morning train, which has an extra van for the branch parcels traffic. The Class E4 had begun life as GER Class T26, which were often called 'Intermediates'. There were very few kinds of GER train which they never worked, as originally they totalled 100, and were spread throughout the system.

Plate 21 (above): Two glories of Ely, the cathedral and a 'Claud Hamilton' locomotive. In fact, No. 62558 had been modernised several times since 1906 when it was built as GER Class D56, and was eventually scrapped in 1957, a year after this picture. The reversed named train headboard is from an earlier working, while the leading coach, with its long grab handles and LNER fitted vacuum pipe under the footboard, is also GER.

Plate 22 (below): On Whit Saturday of 1956, No. 62553 makes a very smoky exit from the east end of Ely Station with a train to March. As can be seen from its length, the level crossing gate did not attempt to block all the lines when it was open for road traffic and, indeed, the main road had been diverted to pass beneath the line by a bridge, so the crossing was little used.

Plate 23: Two local stalwarts, a Class J15 and a 'Claud Hamilton', outside the rather delapidated shed at Bury St. Edmunds in September 1953. Little sheds like this were once a common feature of the British railway scene, each with a few engines of uncertain age, looked after by a small and dedicated staff. Any town possessing such an establishment had, in consequence, a slight but definite railway community, a distinct element in the town's life. New forms of traction and branch line closures swept them all away.

Plate 24: A regular interval service of trains from Liverpool Street to Clacton and Walton was introduced in the 1950 summer service, and eight years later the Walton portion of the 10.36a.m. from London was taken over at Thorpe-le-Soken, where the train divided, by a 45 year old 0-6-0, No. 65470 of Class J15. No doubt it was economical rostering, but it didn't say much for the prestige of the service.

Plate 25: The start of a pilgrimage. At the far end of the suburban area was the Epping to Ongar line, latterly part of London Transport, but still with oil lamps and GER steam engines. In this picture, a pair of Class F5 2-4-2 tanks wait for duty outside the modern shed at Epping in 1956. On the left there is a glimpse of the little used turntable, while the brake van of the branch train is on the right.

Plate 26: A sister engine to those in *Plates 13 & 25*, No. 67193, with a wartime stovepipe chimney, calls at the remote Blake Hall Station. The coaches are LNER, and the poster proclaims 'Harwich for the Continent'. There is space for double track, but the traffic never developed to require it.

Plate 27 (left): No. 62592, with its polished smokebox ring, was someone's favourite 'Claud Hamilton', is pictured coasting towards Yarmouth (Vauxhall) with a lightweight train from Norwich. The coaches are LNER, and the flat and featureless landscape is typical of this part of East Norfolk.

Plate 28 (above): By 1956, Great Eastern engines had penetrated the enemy camp at Yarmouth (Beach). Here, with a GWR coach leading, No. 62533 works the 10.33a.m. train to Peterborough, via the M&GN route, a trip that took four hours. On Saturdays it took even longer!

Plate 29 (below): Lines in East Anglia have long been in peril, but steam was still secure in the 1950s. In this view, a former GNR 4-4-2 tank enters St. Olaves with the 11.40a.m. local train from Yarmouth (South Town) to Beccles. The station still has oil lamps. After leaving St. Olaves, this service will cross the swingbridge over the River Waveney, and then take the right hand fork at Swing Bridge Junction to climb over the line from Norwich to Lowestoft, which passes underneath at Haddiscoe (High Level).

Plate 30: On a cold, bright day in the early spring of 1956, the strengthening sun picks out the bare branches of the trees and casts the shadows of barrow, gas lamp, and footbridge on the platform at Beccles, where a very travel-stained Class J15 has just arrived with a local train. This was one of the places without a turntable, so the tender cab would have made the return journey a little easier on this chilly day. In the 1950s, Beccles was still a junction, even if of only limited importance, with lines going east to Lowestoft, north to Yarmouth and Norwich, and west to Tivetshall, via the Waveney Valley line.

Plate 31: A leaky Class J17 (GER Class G58) No. 65558, wheezes out of Lowestoft with a local goods train. The meagre platform and waiting facilities, on the right, were not for excursionists, but had something to do with Lowestoft's once booming fish traffic.

Plate 32: The Norfolk & Suffolk Joint line was a child of East Anglian railway politics, being Great Eastern and Midland & Great Northern Joint (Joint). By 1956, it was BR Eastern Region, and no one heeded its ancestry. The shuttle from Lowestoft Central to Yarmouth (South Town) pulls away from Coke Ovens Junction at Lowestoft behind F6 class No. 67234. The next stop will be Lowestoft (North).

Plate 33: A broadside view of a 'Battleship', this being a Class A5 locomotive built for the GCR, pictured at Lowestoft in April 1956. The very deep main frames at the front end were a feature of Robinson-designed engines.

Plate 34 (right upper): Class E4 No. 62797 has a tender cab, to make life easier on its frequent tender first workings from Lowestoft, where it posed for a picture on shed. Despite being, as a tender 2-4-0, something of an anachronism in 1956, it still possessed a certain dignity.

Plate 35 (right lower): King's Lynn was a terminus, and there was much changing of engines there as trains reversed to go on their way. Happily, for the photographer, this meant an abundance of GER types. In this view, Class D16 No. 62522 sets out with an early morning train in April 1956, and passes some nice relics of GER passenger stock from the 1890s, which are visible on the right.

Plate 36 (above): After reversing at King's Lynn, the 2.24p.m. service from Liverpool Street was provided with Class J19 No. 64669 for the last stage of its journey, 'all stations' to Hunstanton. Thirty seven minutes were allowed for the 15 miles, so even a goods engine should not have been unduly pressed to keep time.

Plate 37: The frosty morning air shows up every wisp of escaping steam, as Class J17 No. 65501 sets off from its base at King's Lynn with a goods train in 1956. The very varied load is typical of local goods trains of that era, in the last decade when it was possible to see them everywhere.

Plate 38: For goods traffic to East Anglia, March was the key, and here, No. 65577 rumbles in over the crossing at March East Junction with a train bound for the marshalling yard. This class (J17) was the goods equivalent of a 'Claud Hamilton' in its day. Footbridge, signal box, and signals are all GER, while on the left is part of the original Eastern Counties Railway station of 1847.

Plate 39: The Class J20 locomotives were the last development of GER goods power, contemporary with the 1500 (B12) class, and like them were given round-topped boilers. In this photograph, No. 64683 is using the line around the passenger station at March, and heading south towards Ely. It was built in 1922 as GER Class D81.

Plate 40: The setting sun catches No. 62511 as it leaves Yarmouth (Vauxhall) with a five coach load, as No. 62613 waits to back down on to another train. There was a local code of discs to indicate routeing in this area, where there were many lines and junctions. In the foreground is a reminder of the extensive signalling equipment associated with a manual signal box at a busy station.

Plate 41: Looking out from under the 1860-built all-over roof at Aldeburgh, we can see a Class F6 engine just arriving with the branch train from Saxmundham. After 95 years of use, the roof, although dark and cavernous, was still in reasonable condition, and welcome when the east winds blew in from the sea. The engine is about to uncouple, run round its train using the points just visible, and propel the coaches back under the cover of the roof prior to returning to Saxmundham.

Plate 42: On the main line to Ipswich is Mark's Tey, where a long straggling branch from Cambridge once came in. Colchester to Cambridge trains were often worked by Class J15 locomotives, and in May 1956 No. 65456 was just running on to the junction points. The next stop will be Chappel & Wakes Colne.

Plate 43: Before reaching the first station on the journey to Cambridge, the branch crossed the lofty brick viaduct over the Colne Valley. No. 65390 is pictured with a train from Cambridge, and still carries the extra lamp iron on the offside, which it acquired when working on the Midland Railway's line from Cambridge to Kettering.

Plate 44: Chappel & Wakes Colne was the junction for the former Colne Valley & Halstead Railway, where No. 65438 was the Colne Valley line engine in 1956. The driver has just given up the staff, and is about to receive the tablet for the section to Mark's Tey. The train is using the wrong platform so that a train from Cambridge, via the Long Melford line, can be accepted by the signalman before this train has gone forward into the section ahead.

Plate 45: Witham, in Essex, was once the focus of a number of cross-country lines, by which it was possible to do an 'outer circle' journey from Southend to Bishop's Stortford. By the 1950s there were only two stumps left, from Witham to Maldon and Braintree. The wooden trestle bridges were a novelty on the Maldon line, and imparted something of a 'Wild West' flavour to rural Essex, while the fire bucket, on its post just behind the train, is quite in keeping. The engine carries no headcode for its amble down the branch, but still has the brackets on the smokebox for destination boards once carried in the London area.

Plate 46: On the Braintree branch, Class F5 No. 67221, with its side-windowed cab, stops at Cressing in Essex. The platform awning, with decorated valance and brackets, is a charming feature. This station was opened in 1862, and had changed little when this picture was taken in 1956.

Plate 47: In the spring of 1956, electrification work was taking place at Southend (Victoria), so the crew of No. 61575 was keeping a sharp look-out as they brought their train in from London. All the Class B12s on the GER section carried the large round-topped boilers, as fitted in the 1930s.

Chapter Two   Great Northern

When writing in *Chapter III* about the Great Central Railway, I term King's Cross a gateway, and that's just what it was for me. Far more than any other station, it was the gateway to the North but, of course, that is purely a personal and subjective view, and in this chapter it must be merely the gateway to the GNR. Gateway or not, like most large terminal stations, it was a difficult place in which to take pictures without special permission. I have yet again had to stretch the term pre-grouping to include an engine built by the LNER to a Great Northern design, and also to do a little trespassing to provide a King's Cross-related picture for this chapter. In this instance *(Plate 48)* 'The Drain' had claimed another victim, and the porter on the platform could do nothing to help the engine crew. They did get away after a struggle. I remember their plight, in full view of many colleagues, which was not a subject for mirth or derision, but sympathy. Maybe many of the enginemen looking on had themselves been caught in that awkward spot on the Moorgate Suburban line.

The train in the picture came only from Moorgate of course, but GNR engines were among the few pre-grouping types which worked right across London to the Southern Railway with goods traffic. Several of them are shown here, the Class J50 specially introduced into the London area for this work, being more powerful than the Class N1. These cross-London trips did not penetrate very far into SR territory, Feltham being generally the furthest destination. On the Southern electric system, freight trains were prohibited

during the morning and evening rush hours, and if there was a delay on the outward journey, which caused the 'foreign' engine to be impounded at its destination, it could not return home until the 'closed period' was over. What happened to a crew thus stranded far from home, I don't know. Presumably they either got paid overtime, or relief men were sent out to take over. As far as the GNR section was concerned quite a lot of traffic was worked by way of King's Cross (York Road), the Metropolitan widened lines and the incline up from the depths at Holborn Viaduct. The gradient is 1 in 40, even steeper than 'The Drain', but a banker was provided there and in any case the line is straight and not entirely in a single line tunnel. The transfer trips from the Great Western Railway to Smithfield involved a considerable mileage in the tunnels of the Inner Circle, and the condensing gear fitted to GWR engines was generally used. In theory, GNR engines should also have condensed their exhausts between King's Cross and Snow Hill but, as much of the route over the widened lines was opened to the sky, I suspect they didn't bother. When the Class J50s were introduced, they had no condensing gear anyway.

Not living in the West Riding, I didn't often think of the GNR as a line of steep gradients, but rather of long ones like Stoke Bank. As it happened there were some pretty difficult climbs in the London area, although they were short. 'The Drain' was the worst, but every 'down' train had to make its way through the tunnels to Finsbury Park. I have one special memory of them. In the hope of seeing more trains, I was going out to the second station on the main line, Harringay, in one of the notorious Great Northern Railway gas-lit sets, hauled by a Class N2. Starting from the suburban platforms at King's Cross, we ran parallel with a main line train in Gasworks Tunnel through which, at the risk of suffocation, I had the window down to see what engine was at its head, and was pleased to record an Ivatt Atlantic. Following my shutting of the window we stopped at Finsbury Park, and very soon I could hear the noise of the approaching express. Naturally I looked out to enjoy the scene as it accelerated through the station, and was greatly surprised to see not one Atlantic but two. It was the only time I ever saw such a thing here, and strangely enough my only other similar experience was on the Brighton line, where the LB&SCR Atlantics derived from the GNR types were daily friends of mine. Alas, by the time I started taking pictures, all the GNR Atlantics had been scrapped, but I treasure the memory of that double-header.

Finsbury Park in its time had been the Great Northern's Clapham Junction, with a fan of branches penetrating the Northern Heights beyond Highgate. By the 1950s, all but one of the services which formerly congregated there had been withdrawn, the sole survivor being the service through Highgate to Alexandra Palace, the 'Ally Pally' branch. When I first knew it there were GCR 2-4-2 tanks which were succeeded, I think, by the GNR Class C12 4-4-2 tanks and, by the time I had a camera, GER Class N7 0-6-2 tanks were working the push-pull service. There were few trains and few passengers to ride on them, and with only a two coach load the Class N7s made light work of the 1 in 80 gradients.

I suppose the Class C12s must have been fairly robust engines because they worked the London suburban traffic before the 0-6-2 tanks came, and also coped with the severe ups and downs of the West Riding. I have only one picture of them there, proudly working a semi-fast service to Bradford before the diesel multiple units took over. When they had been displaced from London, they were sent to other parts of the GNR system, including the Stamford to Essendine branch, and were still there in 1956. On a bright morning they made some fine pictures, but I was somewhat surprised a little later when one boldly appeared on the branch goods service, as I always thought of them as passenger engines. Both the GER and NER sections had examples, the ones at Hull being residents of long standing.

None of the Great Northern express passenger engines survived long enough in regular service for me to get a respectable picture of one, and even in the late 1940s the 4-4-0 locomotives were seldom seen in the London area. Indeed, the only GNR types that were common there, in the sense that a visitor woud certainly see one, were the 0-6-0 and 0-6-2 tanks. The goods tender engines were, in my experience, rare. As so often happens one neglected to take pictures of the commonplace near home, preferring to go further afield in search of novelty. It was this that led me to the Nottinghamshire lines, where the last class of 0-6-0 locomotives were active on passenger work. I chose Basford as a likely looking spot on the map and was well rewarded because, as well as lots of pre-grouping stock on goods trains, there was a regular, if not frequent, passenger service, mostly worked by Class J6 engines. They were turned at the end of their outward journey from Nottingham to Pinxton or Derby, thus avoiding that bugbear of the railway photographer, an engine working tender first.

Although I spent just one day on the Derby line, my 'bag' of Class J6 photographs was impressive, a bonus being the quantity of somersault signals still in use. With gas-lit stations and plenty of other pre-grouping equipment in

sight, the atmosphere was decidedly Great Northern. The coaches were not the gas-lit horrors of the London area, but respectable LNER stock.

When Nigel Gresley moved from the GNR to the LNER he did not, at once, stop the production of engines to the designs of other constituent companies, as the best of them were allowed to multiply in the mid-1920s, and neither did he impose Doncaster details 'wholesale', as Swindon was doing to its new acquisitions. It was, of course, inevitable that when major rebuilding took place, the details of the new portion should have a Doncaster flavour. While the development of other designers' engines ceased with their retirement, Gresley increased and improved his own types, and their GNR ancestry is my excuse for including pictures of Classes 02 and K2, built by the LNER. I have also allowed myself one example of that greatest GNR classic, the A3 Pacific.

Gresley made his name as a carriage designer before he turned to locomotives. The many LNER coaches in these pictures are nearly all his work, and of similar appearance to those built for the GNR in its latter years.

For decades before the Grouping the Great Northern Railway had been 'the foremost line in point of speed' as the Victorians put it, however much it might have been over-shadowed by bigger companies. Sturrock, Stirling and Ivatt saw to that, and Gresley was a worthy upholder of their tradition. Perhaps this is the reason why outsiders like me had an idea of the GNR as a high speed main line, and knew little else. Although they are very far from approaching a geographical coverage of GNR lines, these pictures are a record of my belated attempts to explore the other nature of the Great Northern Railway.

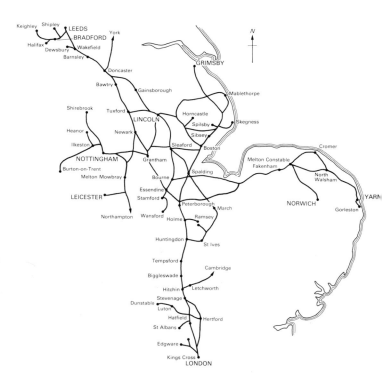

Plate 48: Stalled! Class N2 No. 69544 fails in its attempt to lift an evening business train, from Moorgate to Welwyn Garden City, out of 'The Drain' beside King's Cross. The correct name for this exceedingly treacherous spot was the Hotel Curve, because it passed beneath that gloomy edifice sandwiched between King's Cross and St. Pancras stations: the Great Northern Hotel. On this occasion yet another engine crew had fallen victim to the 1 in 50 gradient. This is the GNR end of the widened lines connection to railways south of the Thames, which are also seen in *Plates 50, 52 and 53.*

Plate 49: On a dull day at Leeds in August 1952, Class C12 No. 67372 has just left Central Station, and proudly carries the express headcode as it approaches Holbeck (High Level) with a light semi-fast working to Bradford. Steam services on this route were an early casualty of diesel multiple units. On the left is that once common feature, the fogman's hut, with the lever and rodding working a detonator placer on the line beneath the engine. On the far left is the joint GNR/NER connection from Geldard Junction *(see Plate 68)*, while the independent LNWR lines are on the right.

Plate 50: One of the LNER-built Class J50 0-6-0 tanks (GNR Class J23) has just crossed the Thames, on a sunny morning in February 1957. The train has come from the GNR line via Farringdon and Snow Hill, and is seen passing Blackfriars Goods Station, formerly a London Chatham & Dover Railway passenger station, on its way to Herne Hill Sorting Sidings. As soon as the widened lines connection with the LCDR opened in 1866, through passenger and goods services from both sides of the river began. The coming of the 'Tubes' in 1907 killed them off. Since 1957, when this picture was taken, towering office blocks have obscured the distant view of St. Paul's.

Plate 51: One of Ivatt's piston valve 0-6-0 locomotives, No. 64235, leaves Kimberley with an afternoon train for Derby (Friargate) in 1957. The somersault signal was a GNR trademark, and although the concrete post may be more modern, there is some evidence to suggest that the GNR used them towards the end of its existence.

Plate 52: The Ivatt Class N1 locomotives were originally London passenger engines, but by June 1952 they were mostly on goods work. Here, No. 69466 is between the tunnels, on the approach to King's Cross, with a load of coal for Hither Green via the widened lines. Belle Isle signal box is in the background, with the North London Railway passing over the bridge behind. The picture was taken from the lines leading to King's Cross Goods and 'Top Shed'.

Plate 53: Homeward bound City office workers look out for their regular companions, as the train from Moorgate emerges into the light at Aldersgate on 13th June 1958. The engine, as for many years past, is a Class N2, but the train is composed of BR compartment stock. With the migration to the West End of so many offices formerly in the City, these services have declined in importance when compared with the period before the war.

Plate 54:   There were few passengers for this Alexandra Palace branch auto-train, pictured at Cranley Gardens in June 1953. In fact, the gardens were beginning to take over the platform, despite the well-kept sign in the distinctive LNER Gill Sans style. The set is branded on the front 'Alexandra Palace Push & Pull', and the leading coach is of GNR stock. Somehow the branch never quite lived up to the hopes of its promoters, and the same was true of the Palace itself. Cranley Gardens Station was only opened in 1902, nearly 30 years after trains first ran on the branch.

Plate 55:   Class N7 tank No. 69692, with the Finsbury Park to Alexandra Palace service at Muswell Hill, is pictured on 25th June 1953. The leading coach, with its long handrails and stubby door handles, is of GER origin, similar to the leading vehicle in Plate 14. The station buildings on the branch were at street level, with stairs down to the platforms, and there was even a goods yard handling coal traffic.

Plate 56: The true King's Cross suburban train, approaching Potters Bar on 15th May 1958, is illustrated by Class N2 No. 69591 at the head of two 'quad-art' sets, the whole scene typifying these services on the GNR line in the London area. On the side of the cutting, just above the bunker, is the City of London monument obelisk marking the boundary of the region inside which a local duty on coal brought in was once payable.

Plate 57: Patrick Stirling was the originator of the GNR saddle tanks which, for many years, handled short distance goods work in the London area. No. 68809 of 1897 was an early example of the Ivatt variety of Class J52, (GNR Class J13) seen here with a dome. By April 1956, when this picture was taken at Spalding, it is unloved and in very poor shape, only a few months away from the scrapyard. Someone has made off with its front numberplate so the number is painted on.

Plate 58: Ivatt's flat-chested Class C12s (GNR Class C2) never looked strong enough for the hills of the West Riding, but they coped there for many years before being transferred to the GNR country branches. The smallish boiler, short smokebox, tall chimney and dome made them look very old-fashioned by 1956, and here No. 67357 has charge of the Stamford to Essendine local train, consisting of one coach and one van, both of a late LNER pattern.

Plate 59: Later in the morning, No. 6735(*(see also Plate 58)* returned from Essendine with what must have been a transfer goods tri for handing over to the London Midland Regio at Stamford. The MR had its own station ther on its Syston & Peterborough line which having been opened in 1848, pre-dated th coming of the GNR by eight years. The LNW section could also be reached at Luffenham, si miles to the west, and using this connectio avoided any congestion at Peterborough, fc traffic coming off the GNR.

Plate 60: A very common combination at a branch line terminus; the passenger station, seen here with an all-over roof, the goods shed, with hand crane outside, and the local gasworks. This is Stamford (East) on the GNR, built in 1856 for the Stamford & Essendine Railway. A century later there were two Class C12s at work. One is pulling out of the station with a shunt, while the other side of the platform is occupied by No. 67357, waiting to go with the train to Essendine.

Plate 61: A GNR signal box at Basford Station, where Class J6 No. 64269 heads a Nottingham to Pinxton train on 5th September 1957. The bridge in the far distance carries the Great Central Railway main line, and a southern connection to the latter at Bagthorpe Junction can be seen curving off to the right between the bridges. The exit from Basford Goods Yard was controlled by a fine set of five miniature somersault signals, all on one post.

Plate 62: Kimberley (GNR) in the late afternoon, with a fine display of pre-grouping equipment on show. Apart from the station and signal box, there are platform seats, gas lamps and, pulled off for the 5.22p.m. Derby (Friargate) to Nottingham (Victoria) service, the 'up' home signal. The engine is Class J6 No. 64202, (GNR Class J22) with LNER stock making up the train.

Plate 63: Built for the War Department in 1918, to a Great Central Railway design, No. 63638 was still earning its keep 40 years later at Kimberley, Nottinghamshire. The goods yard crane with its wooden jib, seen on the right, was once a common sight everywhere, but the portal type loading gauge beneath the overbridge was a rarity. Construction of the deep rock cutting in the background, which leads to Watnall Tunnel, delayed the opening of this line in the 1870s, and for a while only a single line could be used. Without it, the gradients, on what has always been a line principally used by mineral trains, would have been unacceptably severe.

Plate 64: Gresley's modern approach to mixed traffic design was the Class K2 2-6-0 locomotive. In the summer of 1957, No. 61753 makes an impressive sight, treating its train as if it was an express goods on the main line, rather than coal empties bound for a nearby Nottinghamshire colliery. No doubt the crew were taking advantage of the free running ability of their engine, compared with what they could do with a 2-8-0.

Plate 65: Rather more sedate progress at Basford (North) behind another Class J6, this time with a local goods. From the condition of the bottom of the smokebox door, this engine has seen some hard pounding recently, although it survived until 1960, with its Ivatt flat-topped cab, which can be compared with the early Gresley variety seen in *Plate 64*. The ridge of hills pierced at Watnall is in the distance.

Plate 66: The Great Northern Railway was mainly a compact system, leaving 'Empire building', by the acquisition of long penetrating lines, to companies like the Midland Railway. The Nottinghamshire/Derbyshire area was an exception, for in it the GNR thrust out a long tentacle to the west, eventually reaching the LNWR at Stafford. This line was crossed by the Great Central London extension, and between the Class J6 and the rebuilt Class 04 seen in the picture, is a joint connection from Basford West Junction to Bulwell South Junction. Where the GNR and the MR met hereabouts, they studiously ignored one another.

Plate 67: A GCR Class A5 tank at work, on the GNR's Nottinghamshire lines, in September 1957. The GNR/GCR connection at Basford, seen in *Plate 66*, passes behind the signal box. This view shows the coal cage on the bunker which many of these large tanks carried, and can be compared with the NER variety seen in *Plate 125*. The leading coach, with its rectangular mouldings, is older than the other three, but all are LNER.

Plate 68:   A Class A3, with the 'up' 'Queen of Scots' Pullman, slows for the 20m.p.h. restriction past Geldard Junction box, by Holbeck (Low Level), on its way up to Leeds (Central). There it will reverse and pass through Holbeck (High Level), on its way to King's Cross. The lower quadrant signals are NER and the platform on the left is the MR's Holbeck Station, on its main line from St. Pancras to Carlisle. In the distance are the upper quadrant signals of Wortley Junction.

Plate 69:   The GNR had running powers over the NER from Shaftholme Junction to York, and one of Doncaster's Class 02 locomotives was exercising its rights with a through train of hoppers at Selby in 1952. With this 2-8-0 class, Gresley initiated his conjugated valve gear for three cylinders in 1918. No. 63968 was built as late as 1942 and, with its side window cab and a second-hand tender off a Class D49 'Shire', it doesn't look particularly Great Northern. Behind it is a glimpse of the old North Eastern Railway, a clerestory brake from the Goole branch train.

To encounter the Great Central Railway from south of the Thames was a slightly peculiar experience. One met with the extreme end of a main line and only that; just a pair of tracks leading northwards. Other terminals like King's Cross for example, were quite different, for they were gateways to their own territory with the space on either side of the main line filled and taken possession of by branches. However, beyond Marylebone, there was no Great Central territory; indeed the GCR didn't properly start until Quainton Road, 44 miles out, and there were no real branches until well north of Nottingham. The London extension was just that; a single thread of line through the countryside.

At the southern extremity, the GCR atmosphere in the 1950s was pretty thin. The Class L1 tanks had driven out the Class A5s which were built for the suburban traffic, while long distance trains were in the hands of LNER-designed locomotives. Only at Neasden and out on the Chesham branch were pre-grouping engines to be seen. I suspect there were few GCR enthusiasts in London, and to those of us from south of the river it was largely an unvisited line.

Further north, of course, it was different. The old Manchester, Sheffield & Lincolnshire Railway had established itself firmly on both sides of the Pennines, and indeed was early in forcing a crossing of them. But even so there was no true 'GCR country' because it was forced to share Lincolnshire, Yorkshire, Lancashire and Nottingham with the GNR, the L&YR, the LNW and that railway octopus, the MR. Actually the MS&L, in Watkin's time, had itself tried to be an 'octopus', pricking the LNWR in its historic Lancashire heartland at Wigan and St. Helens, and even nibbling at the GWR's extremeties at Chester and Wrexham. Financially undernourished, the MS&L had done this by luring concerns which should have known better, the GNR and the MR, into financing the Cheshire Lines Committee and using that as a springboard to dive into the Lancashire and Flintshire coalfields. It was a typical piece of 'Watkinism', but all that was long ago. In a sense, the London extension was the last, the biggest, and the nearly fatal grasp of the old 'octopus', and typically the GCR only managed to reach London over lines joint with the Metropolitan Railway and the GWR, with which it struck up a 20th century friendship.

The first taste of the Great Central Railway seemed to me to be the shed at Neasden, where the odd Class N5 tank was to be found and, indeed, my only London extension picture was taken there, of the mighty Class L3 2-6-4 tank. The latter amply serves to introduce the 'Battleship' approach to tank engine design. In the decade before the Grouping, various companies suffered an outburst of large and powerful tank engines, mostly six-coupled. With few exceptions (like the GWR) most of the new designs looked and, in fact, were massively heavy, and the GCR representatives were no different. Precisely why the big tanks of this generation made such a gigantic impression I don't know, but the comparison with contemporary 'Battleships' is by no means fanciful. The two classes shown here were obviously brothers. Indeed, I used to think that the Class L3 was created by turning the Class A5 design end to end, and reducing the coupled wheels. However, the admirable RCTS history of the class tells how, in fact, they were based on an LD&ECR 0-6-4 tank design, enlarged with a leading pony truck. World War I killed off the coal shipment traffic to Immingham for which they were built, and

although they could move heavy loads up the Pennine banks, they couldn't stop them coming down the other side, and so the potential of these big tanks was never realised. Happily, the Class A5s didn't suffer the same frustrated existence . After leaving the London area, they found their way to several other parts of the LNER. The one at Darlington is a representative of the 1925 LNER batch, which joined NER 4-4-4 tanks on the County Durham passenger services between the main line and the coast. Of the other pictures, one is on the GER at Lowestoft and the other is working over the GNR Nottingham to Derby line. They were useful engines, although their considerable power saw less and less use in the 1950s until, in the end, the diesel multiple units took over.

The Great Central Railway first reached London over the tracks of the Metropolitan Railway. After the retirement of certain warring parties, relations between the GCR and the Metropolitan were generally harmonious, and their London suburban business grew steadily. Such traffic was no new experience for the company, as for many years it had been developing similar services in the Manchester area, both on its own and on joint lines.

This traffic was worked, until the early 1950s, by the Robinson 4-4-2 tanks. Although of much slighter of appearance than the Class A5s which took over from them in London, they were renowned for their feats of acceleration. These were hardly required on the Chesham branch, but a superheated Class C13 leaving Manchester (London Road) could give any LMS 2-6-4 tank something to think about when it came to getting its train on the move.

For the seeker of GCR engines in the early 1950s, the Manchester area was most rewarding. The Manchester

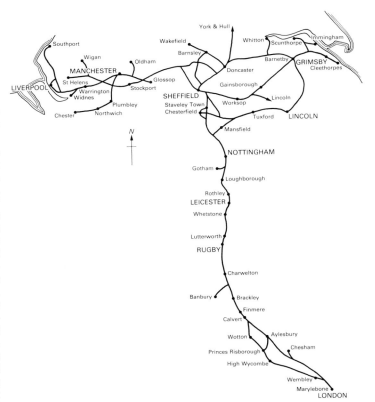

(London Road) suburban services were ones where GCR influence was strong and the Cheshire Lines services were another, providing a feast in the shape of the 'Director' class, the last surviving express design. However, GCR carriages were, in my recollection, very much rarer and in fact, I think there is only one featured in these pictures. My first visit to the CLC was brief but appetising, and I returned in the two following years. Trains at Manchester (Central) were still largely worked by pre-grouping types, and to someone from Sussex, for whom they were a considerable rarity, the appearance of 'Director' class engines on so many trains was very exciting. A trip to Liverpool revealed that there were places along the lineside which were accessible without difficulty, and where photography was possible. The most useful place was inside the triangle of junctions, west of Glazebrook, where the GCR lines to Wigan and St. Helens left the CLC. Here one of the more surprising sights of 1953 was a 'Director' going up the Wigan branch and, in due course, returning tender first. Carriages on the CLC were not obviously pre-grouping, and to an untutored observer they seemed a blend of LMS and LNER style, neat but somehow unremarkable; perhaps I expected prodigies like the engines. However, there were lots of other ways in which the CLC was different. For example, its own brand of signals was still quite common, and so also were things like signs and notices. Even the gloomy cavern of Liverpool (Central) contributed a photograph, and the great arch of Manchester (Central) puts in an appearance. I hope the connoisseurs will be able to pick out significant details for their delight, as I, a stranger, can only point out what struck me, as unusual and interesting.

One of the benefits of forsaking the terminals for the lineside was the goods traffic, and the pick-up goods train was still a normal part of railway working, offering duty for the older generations of engines. By the 1950s there was not a lot left of the MS&L, but the Class J10 goods and the Class N5 tanks were of that creation. As both had a fair turn of speed, they could be used on stopping passenger trains without getting too much in the way, and with their tall domes and long chimneys, albeit the dreadful 'flowerpot', they were a pleasant survival. The Belpaire fireboxes, which looked somewhat out of place with the Victorian boiler mountings were, in fact, among the earliest on an English railway. Their passenger train counterparts had long since been scrapped.

The chimneys carried by Great Central engines in BR days were a mixed bag, which was a pity, because the chimney very much sets the tone where looks are concerned. I never saw anything with the Parker/Pollitt stovepipe version, but the results of LNER sensibilities were prominent. One was happy the other was not. The older engines in these pictures are all suffering under the despised 'flowerpot', but why such a terrible thing was done to them, when a perfectly respectable chimney could be produced for the Class J11 'Pom-Poms', I don't know. However, the LNER seemed to recognise that if the 'long flowerpot' looked unhappy on the small GCR engines, the 'short flowerpot' looked even worse on the large ones. Around 1930, Gorton produced an LNER chimney which only the knowledgeable could tell from the original, and honour was satisfied, as it was a nice compliment to Robinson's artistry; GCR engines were usually well-proportioned.

Another Gresley compliment to Robinson was the production of further examples of his work in the mid-1920s. The Class A5s for the North Eastern Area have already been mentioned, and in 1924 two dozen 'Improved Director' locomotives were built for use on the North British section. I have thought it proper to include a picture of each of these LNER series. The greatest testimonial to a Robinson design came earlier, during World War I, when one was selected as the Railway Operating Division standard heavy goods engine. Many hundreds of Class 04 engines were built, of which the LNER bought 273 to add to the GCR originals. The class went through many detail changes, mainly concerning the boilers, but it is a proof of how much the front end determines an engine's appearance, that only those which lost their Robinson smokebox and chimney looked notably different. Happily one has been preserved, as has a 'Director', so both of Robinson's most successful designs are still with us. As one would expect, the Class 04s were found mainly in the coalfield area. These engines were worthy representatives of a railway which, in this century, when Sam Fay took it in hand, did things in style. A Class C13 raising the echoes leaving Manchester (London Road), a 'Director' sailing along at 70m.p.h. apparently without effort with a Manchester to Liverpool fast, and a Class 04 in charge of an unending procession of coal wagons were, in their different ways, all exemplars of Great Central Railway style.

Plate 70: One of the monster Class L3 tanks at Neasden in 1952, where it was working out its time before withdrawal the following year. These engines, as GCR Class 1B, were the first British 2-6-4 tanks. Although designed after the A5 4-6-2 tanks, they were not just a goods version of them.

Plate 71: A Class 04 2-8-0 passing Staveley (Central) on the GCR main line with 30 loaded coal wagons, a typical duty in the autumn of 1957. The engine is just passing over the points, by which the Chesterfield loop line diverges to form a four track section into Staveley Station, before going off to the west. Although built for the ROD, the GCR outline of this engine is unmistakable. They were GCR Class 8K, sometimes nicknamed 'Tinies'.

Plate 72: The pre-Robinson style. No. 69263 was built for the MS&L in 1893, and was still at work 64 years later. It was LNER Class N5,(GCR Class 9C). In the background is another relic of a vanished railway scene: the slatted wooden extension fitted to a mineral wagon to increase its capacity when carrying coke. Looking at the engine's chimney, one can see from where the nickname 'flowerpot' came.

Plate 73 (above): The Metropolitan and Great Central railways' alliance continued into the 1950s, with Class C13 4-4-2 tanks working the Chalfont to Chesham push-pull trains. No. 67416 has just arrived at Chesham in June 1958 but, despite the signs, the atmosphere was not at all London Transport. Like the signal and the signal box, it was Metropolitan Railway, and well merits the publicists description; 'A sunny day in Metroland'.

Plate 74 (below): The Great Central Railway main line was worked by a considerable variety of engines in the autumn of 1957. Among them was Colwick's Class J6 No. 64269, with the 10.08a.m. 'all stations' train from Sheffield (Victoria) to Nottingham (Victoria), which was composed of four bogies, two vans and a horsebox. The infrequent stopping trains on the main line had to deal with every variety of traffic, however miscellaneous, so the station time allowed was considerable, and this train took nearly two hours to travel just over 70 miles. The GCR signal box is Staveley Town North. Note the fogman's hut which is tipped over and out of use.

Plate 75 (right upper): One of the Railw Operating Division (ROD) 2-8-0s, of World Wa vintage, is flanked by its World War II count parts, the WD (War Department) class, at Colw in 1957. The fitting of a round-topped boiler h made little difference to its looks. What we c see, however, is evidence of the changing ide about the external appearance of the locomoti the way, even in wartime, the older generation designers did not sacrifice a tidy and relativ smooth appearance to the needs of speedy prod tion. By the 1940s there was no such concern looks, but a greater regard for ease of servicing. British eyes the WD looked decidedly American.

Plate 76 (right lower): A short train of emp mineral wagons in North Derbyshire. The engi is Class J11 (GCR Class 9J), and the scene is the GCR main line just north of Staveley (Centra Competition here came from the Midland Railwa and its line passed under the GCR about where t brake van of this train stands. The line on t right, protected by what looks like a GCR sign on a concrete post, served a local pit, and not make connection with the enemy. The ma line signals are 'off' for a through train, wh the subsidiary home and distant signals are for t Chesterfield loop, which begins its independe existence north of the station. The line on the left a headshunt for the local marshalling yard whi catered for the extensive coal traffic.

Plate 77: The 9.24a.m. Chesterfield (Central) to Sheffield (Victoria) local train leaves the loop line platform at Staveley (Central) on 6th September 1957. The GCR had a habit of calling their stations 'Central' or 'Town', when a competing railway also served the same location. Someone in BR carried on this habit, because both the GCR and the LNER had called the location shown here Staveley (Town), as we can see from the signal box which is shown in *Plate 74*. The next two stations to the north also acquired the suffix 'Central', to distinguish them from the former LMS stations on the MR line. The engine is a Robinson Class C13 No. 67424, and the coaches are post-Gresley LNER.

Plate 78: The Oldham, Ashton & Guide Bridge Joint line push-pull service at Oldham (Clegg Street), in March 1955. No. 67421 is a member of Class C13 (GCR Class 9K), and the leading coach is also GCR, dating from the early years of this century. The service over this line, which was originally LNWR and GCR Joint property, threaded its way through what can only be described as the eastern back streets of the railway network in the Manchester area, and provided a useful local connecting link. By the 1950s, cotton manufacture, which had been the staple industry of the district, was fading fast, but the mill chimneys and their smoke were still much in evidence.

Plate 79: LNER Class S1, (GCR Class 8H) one of the GCR 0-8-4 tanks, built in 1907 for hump shunting at Wath. These huge machines were not often found elsewhere, but in 1951 the first representative of the class was at Gorton, for the fitting of a superheater. Like all of Robinson's later engines, it has the large oval buffers. The wheel and handle fastening for the smokebox door has been replaced by twin handles, and the shapely Robinson dome and chimney have also been replaced.

Plate 80: A Manchester area suburban train for Glossop leaves the GCR side of Manchester (London Road) Station, (now called Piccadilly). The burnt smokebox door is evidence of how sorely tried the Class C13 engines were in their last years on these services. The vehicle on the right, with recessed door handles, is a late GCR full brake by Robinson, whose carriages looked as good as his engines.

Plate 81: The great arched roof of Manchester (Central) Station was related to its more famous counterpart at St. Pancras, and makes an interesting contrast with the less spectacular roof of Manchester (London Road), seen under repair in *Plate 80*. In this picture, the very first of the 'Director' or D10 class (GCR Class 11E) is leaving with a stopping train to Chester (Northgate), a rather humble duty 40 years after it was built as the pride of the line in 1913. Despite this, someone appreciated its looks enough to keep it clean and to polish the splasher beading.

Plate 82: An 'Improved Director' class was built from 1919 onwards, and they could easily be distinguished from the earlier engines by their side-windowed cabs. They were classified D11 (GCR Class 11F), and in this picture at Manchester (Central) we can see both varieties. No. 62666 *Zeebrugge* has been well-polished before bringing empty stock into the terminus in the summer of 1952. The older engine is in the background.

Plate 83: The Class C13 tanks shared the CLC workings to Chester with the 'Director' class, and it would appear that the driver of No. 67436 did not relish making the 39 mile journey bunker first, so he made use of the vacuum-powered turntable adjoining Manchester (Central). The background of warehouse and gas holder is suitably commercial for Manchester, while a clean Class B1 seems determined to add to the grimy condition of its surroundings. The long smokebox of the C13, set well forward, gives the engine a purposeful look when compared with the Ivatt Class C12s on the GNR.

Plate 84: In August 1953 it was still possible to see 0-6-0s at the head of a substantial goods train. No. 64322 typifies such workings and is seen at Irlam on the CLC main line. This engine was, in fact, a product of the 20th century, and a member of Class J11 (GCR Class 9J) which enjoyed enduring popularity. With the London Midland Region take-over of CLC motive power responsibility after Nationalisation, the J11s were all transferred away from CLC sheds to the Eastern Region but, nevertheless, continued to be seen between Liverpool and Manchester. Irlam is on the eastern half of the CLC main line and, when this picture was taken, it still had one of the very distinctive CLC style station nameboards.

Plate 85: Although former LMS engines were responsible for most of the CLC express workings, Trafford Park shed turned out No. 62668 *Jutland* for a lightly-loaded Liverpool to Manchester duty on 26th August 1952. With a train weighing under 200 tons, and an easy road, this 'Director' class engine didn't have to be worked hard to sweep down the short incline from the bridge over the Manchester Ship Canal to the west of Flixton, and past the camera with a speed exceeding 70m.p.h.

Plate 86: This short train stopping at Irlam in the summer of 1953, was the midday service from Manchester (Central) to Wigan (Central). It is headed by a Class N5 0-6-tank, one of over 100 built jointly between 1891 and 1901 by Gorton Works and Beyer Peacock & Co. at the nearby Gorton Foundry. The cast-iron sign and the CLC signal remind us of past ownership, which was still a recent memory.

Plate 87: A Manchester (Central) to Liverpool (Central) stopping train leaves Glazebrook on the CLC main line in August 1953. The station platform is just visible on the left beyond the bridge, above which we can see Glazebrook West Junction signal box. The East Junction is at the far end of the station, and controls the junction with the line to Stockport (Tiviot Dale). On this side of the bridge the line to Wigan (Central) turns away to the left, behind the characteristic CLC signal. The six coach train is composed of CLC stock, and is headed by one of the earlier series of 'Director' engines, No. 62656 *Sir Clement Royds*.

Plate 88: Looking northwards across the plain towards the line of the Liverpool & Manchester Railway, we can the second side of the triangle at Glazebrook, with Glazebrook Moss Junction on the Wigan line in the distance. Behind the signals on the extreme left the third side of the triangle runs back south westwards to the main line at Dam Lane Junction. This triangle was actually GCR property, as neither the GNR or MR, the other partners in the CLC, were willing to get involved in 'Watkinite' expeditions into Lancashire, however glowing the prospects might be. All this was in the days of the Manchester, Sheffield & Lincolnshire Railway, and it is fitting that the Class J10 engine on the pick-up goods from Wigan was of that company's design, subsequently GCR Class 9D. The harvest was good in 1953, as we can see!

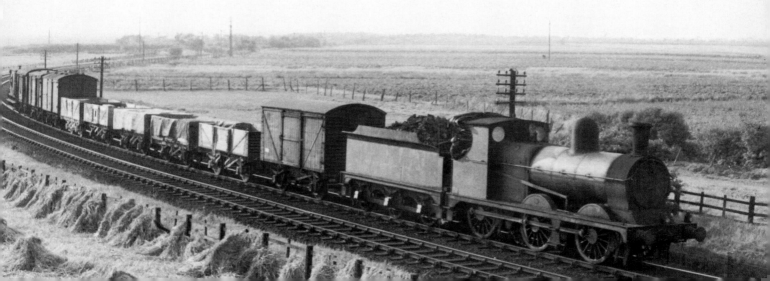

Plate 89: The Merseyside sun makes a rare appearance in Liverpool (Central) Station during August 1951, and catches one of the J11 class locomotives while on an empty stock working. This engine, No. 64420, was one of a number which were rebuilt from 1942 onwards with piston valves, as part of the plan to make them an LNER standard design. A consequence of this rebuilding was that the boilers were set higher in the frames, and had shorter chimneys. The whole class was nicknamed 'Pom-Poms' from the beginning, because their sharp exhaust reminded some returned Boer War veteran of the sound of a quick-firing gun used in South Africa.

Chapter Four   The North Eastern

The North Eastern Railway was a very wealthy concern with some surprising features, and where it was in the public eye, things were done in an ample and even lavish way. This was true of branch lines as well as the main line, but in places where its passengers did not go, one could find some remarkable survivals from the primitive age of railways. I first saw a rope-worked incline from the window of an East Coast express and, when I later began to explore the North Eastern Railway I discovered that endearing backwater, the Stanhope & Tyne Railway. The whole line had been built for rope haulage when the steam locomotive had just superseded such a method in the minds of early railway engineers, and even after conversion to locomotive working many reminders of its past could still be found. It survived for over a century as a relic of the 'Railway Stone Age' but to be more precise, it was a relic of the carboniferous period. Coal was its origin, although the moorland section which reached Stanhope, was in search of limestone and other minerals. A remote branch from this section attained the highest point reached by the standard gauge in England, 1,680ft., at the Bolts Law Engine House above Rookhope. This was on a private line, and not part of the North Eastern Railway, and any explorer of the latter in BR days was bound to come across some of these private mineral lines sooner or later. By the 1950s most of them belonged to the

National Coal Board, and several still had rope-worked inclines. Indeed, the Bowes Railway was largely thus, with ancient and modern meeting in the Team Valley, where the Bowes trucks, on their rope, threaded a way underneath the East Coast Main Line. In fact, BR itself operated at least one similar incline, at Waldridge.

The eastern section of the Stanhope & Tyne Railway climbed from the river to Consett, with its ironworks, some 20 miles away and 800ft. up. By the time I visited this line the iron-ore trains to Consett were worked by BR 2-10-0s, but the NER 0-8-0s were still active. The Stanhope & Tyne's rope-worked past had required deviations to be built for locomotive working, but even these had formidable gradients, although both the Class Q6 and the 3 cylinder version ClassQ7 0-8-0 locomotives tackled them noisily but successfully, with coal empties and other traffic. I recall no passenger trains at all, although Consett was once a local centre served from several directions. Now even the ironworks has gone, but there is a picture of it here with a Class Q6 on duty.

Coal mining today, is almost extinct in County Durham west of the main line. It wasn't exactly flourishing in the 1950s as many pits were nearly worked out, but there was enough coal moving to make it worth a visit, especially as much of the motive power was North Eastern. Washington,

County Durham, looked a good place on the map, so one fine afternoon I made my way there by bus and, as these pictures show, it was a fruitful visit. To me, the Class Q6 0-8-0 locomotives were descendants of Hackworth's engines for the Stockton & Darlington Railway. We had nothing like them in the south, and they were a unique sight coupled to the very distinctive high-sided wooden coal wagons, of which the NER had thousands. Another disturbing novelty was the appearance round the corner of an NCB engine working a train over the BR line.

I could not even imagine the 0-8-0s ever working a passenger train, but the North Eastern also had several hundred 0-6-0s of more familiar type, some of which had once been the company's mixed traffic engines. Their use on a passenger duty was not something I ever managed to photograph. After steam had virtually disappeared from the North Eastern Region, south of the Tyne, the Class J27 0-6-0s were still very active in Northumberland, between the main line and the sea, almost monopolising the goods and mineral workings there. Just as I worked out from a map that Washington might be a good centre for lineside photography, I found Newsham, the focus of a system of lines serving both sides of the River Blyth. There were also passenger trains worked by Class G5 0-4-4 tanks. However, the real magnet was the continuous flow of trains of coal and empties, mostly worked by several sizes of NER goods, with virtually every one containing some of the distinctive coal wagons.

I made my way to Blyth one afternoon to see another special feature of working in the North-East, the great wooden staithes. Each was approached by a steeply-inclined track, at the riverward end of which were the chutes for loading the coal from the bottom-discharge wagons into the holds of ships lying alongside. The attraction was the method of getting the coal trucks up to this loading height, which involved an all-out effort by the engine pushing the loaded wagons. One might have expected that this would be done by some powerful modern type of locomotive, but instead they used various classes of small 0-6-0 tanks. Perhaps the staithes couldn't take the weight of anything heavier. I managed a footplate trip on one of these assaults, and had a rare experience of full regulator, full cut-off working. Some of these shunting engines were distinguished by having been rebuilt from 0-4-4 tanks, and many still possessed a relic of their origins in the shape of their cabs. Whereas other NER engines had cabs of quite normal outline, these early rebuilds sported a bent-over roof variety, with large square spectacle glasses. To anyone knowing the Fletcher outline of North Eastern engines before the Worsdells came, it was a real hint of the past, and not out of place because the original engines (the BTP-Bogie Tank Passenger) had been built by Fletcher in the 1870s.

As might be expected of any line having an extensive coal traffic, the NER possessed many shunting tanks, although much shunting in collieries was done by train engines. A trumpet-shaped brass cover was a standard North Eastern fitting, until pop-valves replaced the Ramsbottom variety. However, it was found on shunting engines that escaping steam from the pop-valves obscured the drivers' view and could be a serious nuisance. After the fabrication of some home-made deflectors to suppress this problem, the brass trumpets were reintroduced. That they had been prudently kept in store when first removed is a possibility, but far more likely is that they were melted down in the brass foundry and new ones had to be made. Wherever the new trumpets came from, the use of a traditional design was another case of the LNER paying compliments to the past, or perhaps one of the results of decentralising authority to the various Areas, where local styles and traditions were not obliterated by Grouping. BR paid the North Eastern a further remarkable compliment by

building another 28 Class J72 0-6-0 tanks between 1949 and 1951, each complete with a brass trumpet.

Although there was much of unusual interest in these coalfield corners of the NER, the principal stations on the main line also had their attractions for a photographer. York was the one I knew first, in the days when the famous NER Class R (D20) 4-4-0 locomotives still worked local trains. York had the advantage of seeing lots of trains, but I suspect that much worthy of a picture escaped me at the station, and used the goods avoiding line. Everthing going south, however, had to pass under Holgate Road Bridge, between the excursion platforms there, which made a perfect grandstand for the photographer.

A lesser-known attraction at York was Derwent Valley Light Railway. Although it retained its independence from the LNER after nationalisation, in the 1950s it was using hired motive power in the shape of a Class J25 0-6-0. One memorable and freezing day in 1955, I made the journey to Cliff Common and back on the footplate. Photographically it wasn't very wonderful, but as pictures on the Derwent Valley seem so rare I have included one here. We were certainly glad that day of the side window cab, which the NER had fitted to its tender engines for many years.

Another useful centre for photography was Selby, where everything passed over the swingbridge and through the station, including Great Northern engines of Doncaster extraction. There was also a local service to Goole, and Selby was on one of the NER's typical secondary cross-country routes, from Leeds to Hull. Some trains worked through, while others did the journey with an interval at Selby, and many of them were worked by the Class D20s. The older Worsdell express engines and the handsome Atlantics had been scrapped by 1950, but the Class D20s found sanctuary for a few years more. Those at York seemed to disappear early in the decade, but as well as those to be seen at Selby,

they were also to be found at Alnmouth where all survivors were, in 1957, working to Newcastle, as well as on the branch to the beautiful station at Alnwick. With its double all-over roof and lavish spaces, Alnwick was a good example of the way the NER used its wealth.

One of the few places where there was any challenge to the NER benevolent monopoly was at Hull. There, in the late 1880s, an alliance of Town and Pit called into being the Hull, Barnsley & West Riding Junction Railway & Dock Company, the Hull & Barnsley Railway for short. The North Eastern swallowed it up just before the Grouping but one H&BR type remained into the 1950s, the Class N13 0-6-2 tank. The line only ever had one Locomotive Superintendent, Matthew Stirling, son of the great Patrick, and true to the family tradition he believed in domeless boilers and wrap-over cabs. The former were replaced in the 1920s, but the cabs survived to distinguish the Hull article from the several varieties of NER 0-6-2 tanks. These were only one of Hull's specialities. In 1952 the last 'Whitby Willie' (Class A6 inside cylinder 4-6-2 tank) was still there, and there were many other pre-grouping engines and carriages. Here I came across the only hounds van I have ever seen and, to contrast with it, there was plenty of late NER stock with the high-arched roofs. Latterly I wished I had gone back to Hull but, in the early 1950s, there were so many places offering photographic opportunities which were not going to last much longer. As every year brought with it the loss of a further proportion of what was left from before 1923, there was rarely time to make second visits. Today, of course, when the post-grouping is as rare as the pre-grouping was then, I sometimes regret not having given that the attention it deserved.

The LNER didn't go in for large scale visual alterations to the engines it inherited. It is true that something nasty happened on the Great Central section, but in general the looks of the locomotives were rarely transformed. This was true to such an extent that we noticed even detail changes. For example, some of the Class D20 engines exchanged their small flat smokebox doors for larger domed ones, while some also got modern flush-sided tenders, which looked odd behind a patently Victorian engine. There were larger changes too. The massive Class A8 passenger tanks were rebuilt from a 4-4-4 tank design, one of the North Eastern's contributions to the 'Battleship' school of tank engine thought. The result was not unhandsome, being stately rather than ponderous and, in the 1950s, Darlington and the coast saw a lot of them. Lastly, I should mention the Class B16 4-6-0, the last NER mixed traffic type. Although the boiler mountings were cut down to clear the LNER load gauge, the result was a success. So too was the replacement by Gresley and Thompson of the inside steam chests and valve gear, with outside steam chests working with Walschaerts gear. The result was different, but not displeasing.

It is fitting that NER engines changed so little under later ownership, because the same was true of the railway as a whole. I doubt if the picture of the small shunting tanks, ranged round the turntable at Middlesbrough Roundhouse on a Sunday morning could, as late as 1956, have been taken anywhere else in the country. This continuity, and the absence of great changes, was understandable, because the North Eastern had been extremely prosperous for many years and it built things to last, which they did. The next time you go to the National Railway Museum look at the NER offices you pass on the road from the station, and you will see what I mean. They speak, with just a trace of pomp, of solid worth and pride, as the North Eastern never forgot it was the home of railways.

Plate 90: Washington Station saw only two passenger trains daily in 1956, but the procession of mineral traffic was almost unending because this was where the former Stanhope & Tyne route crossed the Leamside line. There were also local collieries and factories nearby, and the duty of No. 63396 was a common one; bringing loads of coal out of a nearby pit. The lines behind the engine lead to the station, and eventually to Tyne Dock.

Plate 91: Looking across Crimple Viaduct, near Harrogate, from the footplate of a Class B16 engine working a goods on the Wetherby to Harrogate line in February 1955. The original Leeds Northern Railway route, from Leeds to Stockton, passes underneath, and the two were joined by a steep connection, from Pannal Junction up to Crimple Junction. The latter connection's splitting home signals can be seen by the engine's chimney.

Plate 92: Although it virtually had a monopoly, the North Eastern Railway served its territory well, by running a useful collection of smartly-timed semi-fast services on cross-country routes joining centres of local importance. For many years former express engines worked these lightly loaded trains, after bigger locomotives had taken over their main line duties. In this way the NER's Class R (D20) locomotives outlived the more powerful Atlantics, and No. 62384 still carries express lights when leaving Selby with the 9.45a.m. Leeds to Hull buffet car train in August 1952. It retains the original smokebox door, and the Westinghouse pump sunk into the driving splashers.

Plate 93: Selby's own Class J27, No. 65875, (NER Class P3) clatters through the station with a local working in 1952. It still looks every inch a Darlington design, despite the later smokebox door. Just visible in the distance are the signals controlling the merging of four tracks into two, over the River Ouse swingbridge, north of the station.

Plate 94 (left upper): Class G5 0-4-4 tank No. 67250, (NER Class 0) leaves the bay platform at the south end of Selby with the 9.58a.m. push-pull service to Goole. The East Coast Main Line is to the left of the engine, while the Leeds & Selby line comes in on the far left behind the signal gantry. A Class J77 shunts in the background.

Plate 95 (left lower): Class J77 No. 68406, (NER Class 290) started life as an 0-4-4 tank in 1875, as NER Class BTP, and was rebuilt to an 0-6-0 tank in 1907. The very distinctive cab and deep side framing were still recognisably the work of Edward Fletcher at Selby in August 1952. It is the same class of locomotive as those which shunted the staithes at Blyth, but life at Selby was very much easier.

Plate 96 (above): The engine working seen in *Plate 92* returned to Leeds by taking a stopping train from Hull to Selby, shunting into the bay platform there for a while, and then going forward with the 2.20p.m. 'all-stations' working to Leeds. This picture, taken at Selby in August 1952, shows the engine during this interval at Selby, when connections were made on the other side of the platform with East Coast Main Line trains.

Plate 97 (below): Late in the afternoon another of Selby's Class D20s shunts the empty stock of the 5.13p.m. stopping train from Leeds. The engine has been equipped with a large smokebox door and a rebuilt flush-sided tender. The leading coach, with its square-topped ducket and high-arched roof, is of late North Eastern Railway vintage.

Plate 98: Still with its Westinghouse brake, Class G5 No. **67256** was one of the station pilots at Hull in 1952, seen in this view shunting an NER coach still in LNER livery. Perhaps because it was away from the main line, Hull seemed to have a greater proportion of pre-grouping rolling stock than other places of its size. Also, where else did gas lamps share posts with loudspeakers?

Plate 99: The last Hull & Barnsley engines in existence were 0-6-2 tanks of Class N13 (H&BR Class F3), built by Hawthorn Leslie in 1913/14. The round-topped cabs sweeping back into long bunkers made them very distinctive. No. 69119 was the last to be built and is seen in August 1952 at Springhead Depot, Hull, the heart of the H&BR system. The only other place to have examples of this class was the NER shed at Neville Hill, Leeds.

Plate 100: Another Hull rarity was the last of the Class A6 inside cylinder 4-6-2 tanks (NER Class W). The massive slab-sided look is achieved by the way the side sheeting of the large tanks is continued on to be part of the cab. The chalked '34' on the smokebox door was a local duty or trip number, in the summer of 1952.

Plate 101: The six wheeler behind Class C12 No. 67392 is from the Great Eastern Railway. It may have done many a high speed mile in earlier days but, by 1952, it was being used as a local van. Its low roof matches that of the engine, but it was quite dwarfed by the prosperous looking NER brake third with its continuous row of toplights. In the distance, a Class D49 engine waits to pull out with a train to York. As these pictures show, the NER station at Hull was a considerable establishment, and in the 1950s was still the focus of a widespread network of passenger services in East Yorkshire.

Plate 102: Extra platforms were provided for excursion and race traffic south of Holgate Road Bridge at York and, over the years, photographers have blessed them. On a busy summer Saturday in 1952, a rather grimy Class B16, No. 61478, accelerates hard on the main line to keep out of the way of the heavy express traffic. The fireman has been waiting to get clear of York Station before building up his fire, and the heavy pulling is burning it through nicely. It made a good picture, and no doubt the people who lived close to the line were resigned to the occasional pall of smoke.

Plate 103: The Derwent Valley Light Railway was nearly always worked by engines hired from the NER and its successors. On a freezing day in January 1955, the daily return goods working from York to Cliff Common was in the charge of Class J25 No. 65677, seen here at Cottingwith. Although the passenger service ceased in 1926, the 1940s and 1950s were prosperous for the Derwent Valley, and its stations were well-kept. There was nothing of the Col. Stephens' Light Railway poverty about this line.

Plate 104: Massively handsome and well-shined up, Class A8 No. 69865 from Whitby waits at the north end of York Station, before working a Scarborough line train in 1952. Prior to the time of wholesale closures of small stations, the LNER had acquired an unenviable record for the longest distance between stations, 21¼ miles from York to Malton, by closing every one between those places.

Plate 105: No. 61410, of Class B16 (NER Class S3), runs down towards Leeds with a slow train, near Killingbeck, on 9th March 1955. These engines were equally at home on almost any kind of train, as can be seen by comparing this view with *Plates 102 and 107*, but their power was rather wasted on a local stopping service.

Plate 106: The main girders of the locomotive turntable at Starbeck Shed, Harrogate, were removed to Gorton Works in Manchester to be repaired, and this caused the use of a Class A8 tank on the 'Harrogate Sunday Pullman' in the winter of 1955. In this view, No. 69882 catches the last of the sunshine while crossing The Stray on the approach to Harrogate.

Plate 107: Darlington, like York, was a place where through trains could completely avoid passing through the station, but that was no guarantee of safety, and it did not prevent a disaster in which 25 passengers were killed. On the night of 27th June 1928, a Scarborough to Newcastle passenger train, using the avoiding line, collided head on (at a point on the extreme right of this picture) with another train which had improperly shunted out into its path. On a fine summer evening in August 1956, the driver of No. 61419, heading north with a fast goods train, can see that the road ahead is clear as he passes the platform approach tracks at the south end of the station.

Plate 108:   Edward Thompson rebuilt some of the Class B16 locomotives to improve their running and, in consequence, made them look more modern. No. 61468 was one of the rebuilds, and is seen pulling away on the through lines north of Darlington with a long express goods train in the summer of 1956. The lamp headcode indicates a Class C train, vacuum-braked for at least half its length, compared with a Class D train, only one third braked, as seen in *Plate 107.* Just ahead of the engine is a sign of things to come, marking the site of a new depot to be erected for diesel trains.

Plate 109:   No. 69832 was built, for the LNER by Hawthorn Leslie in 1925, to a GCR design. The Class A5s shared the coast line workings in the North-East with the Class A8s, many of the trains being composed of pairs of articulated coaches as in this view at Darlington. The exemplary tidiness of the permanent way was common hereabouts, a legacy of the pre-war work of John Miller, Civil Engineer of the North Eastern Area.

Plate 110: The North Eastern Railway's last essay in the field of large passenger tanks was a 4-4-4 tank design, Vincent Raven's NER Class D, rebuilt by the LNER to a more useful 4-6-2 tank (Class A8). By the 1950s they were the mainstay of the Darlington—Middlesbrough—Saltburn services, and it is with such a train that No. 69868 arrives at Darlington.

Plates 111 & 112:   No.69869 retains the thick boiler cladding, flush with the smokebox, but No. 69866, seen in *Plate 112,* was more conventionally-equipped. The rear end view emphasises not only the size of these engines but also how small the cab opening was, and shows the elevated driving position. Both engines are at Darlington with trains for the coast.

Plate 113:   The tombstone symbol on the splasher marks the end for Class J71 No. 68255. There were many small varia-
tions among these shunters which made each one worth a detailed study, and here, for example, we can see the organ pipe
whistle, the brass safety-valve trumpet placed over modern pop-valves, a steel and oak sandwich buffer beam, and even the
fittings for the shunting pole, which once lay along the side framing. The setting is as interesting as the engine, for these tracks
were once part of the 'Darlington Depot' of the Stockton & Darlington Railway. Beyond the trees is North Road Station,
Darlington, now a museum.

Plate 114:   Three generations of North Eastern Railway six-coupled power, on shed at Darlington. No. 65033 was one of
the famous 'Superheater C' class express goods engines, (Class J21), Worsdell's first NER goods design and the first with a
side window cab. No. 65829 was one of the last NER 0-6-0s, a P3 (Class J27), while the third generation is represented by
No. 61411, a Class B16 just out of Darlington Works, and the last NER express goods class.

Plate 115: Unlike some of the NER engines still at work in the 1950s, engines of Class J26 (NER Class P2) could never be taken for a Victorian type. In their last years nearly all of the class were to be found on Teesside and in 1956, No. 65758 is seen working a goods train past Thornaby. Everything is typical of the location and the period; rolling stock, traffic (steel plates and coal empties), platforms with neatly bordered flower beds, and signalling. Indeed, every signal visible is of the NER slotted post variety, with the very tall 'half ball and spike' finials similar to those sold by McKenzie & Holland.

Plate 116: We shall not see their like again; a gathering of 0-6-0 shunting pilots resting at Middlesbrough on a Sunday in 1956. They are drawn from the ranks of Classes J71 (NER Class E) and J77 (NER Class 290).

Plate 117: One of BR's surprises was the building of 28 Class J72 tanks between 1949 and 1951, complete with brass safety-valve trumpet, half a century after the type first appeared on the NER as Class E1. No. 69008 was one of these BR engines, its duty in 1956 being banking at Tyne Dock. The antique on the left was one of the shed's tool vans, often the last use of old coaches *(see also Plate 35).*

Plate 118: The NER 0-8-0 locomotives were something of a historical curiosity by the 1950s, and could trace their ancestry back to Timothy Hackworth's engines on the Stockton & Darlington Railway in the morning, if not the dawn, of locomotive history. Working coal traffic to and from Tyne Dock was their earliest employment, and this picture shows Class Q6 (NER Class T2) No. 63429 forging its way up the last few yards of the 1 in 47 gradient from the dock to the main line. The object at the extreme left of the picture is a slotted post signal which has lost its arm, and now stands guard only over the weeds where once there were sidings.

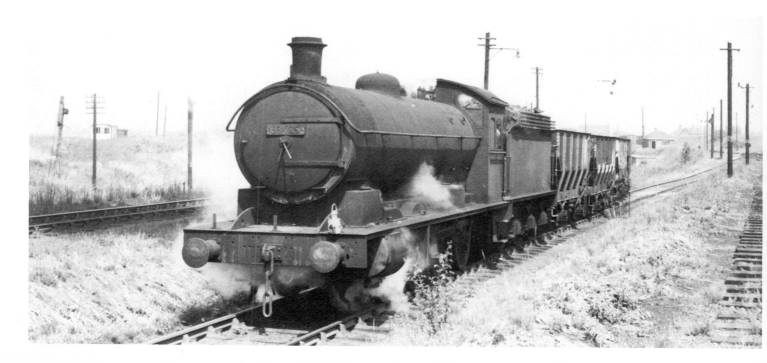

Plate 119: One of the last Class Q6 locomotives to be built, No. 63453, brings a trains of coal empties into Washington, over the line from Penshaw which was opened in 1850. From then until 1872, it was a link in the East Coast route to Scotland. The lines going off to the right are part of the Stanhope & Tyne Railway route towards Stella Gill, also seen in *Plates 121 to 123.*

...ate 120: Built as a two cylinder ...orsdell/von Borries Compound in ...'89, No. 69390 was converted to a ...mple in 1907 and was the last sur-...vor of Class N8 (NER Class B), the ...rge-wheeled version of the NER ...6-2 tank engine shown descending ...e incline in *Plate 121.* In August ...56 it was the engine assigned to look ...ter all local shunting duties at ...ashington. The pipe coming out of ...e frontplate of the cab and leading to ...e smokebox was for the vacuum ...ake. This was fitted by the LNER, ...e NER having been a Westinghouse-...aked line.

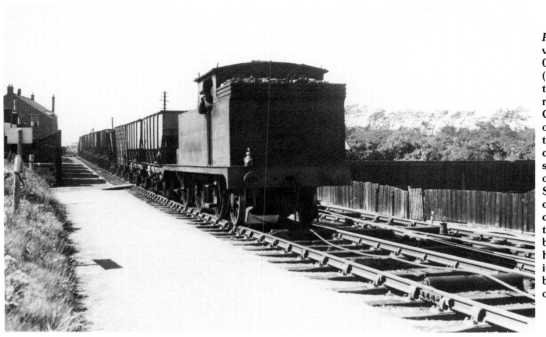

Plate 121: Another of the seven
varieties of North Eastern Railw
0-6-2 tanks, No. 69093 of Class N
(NER Class U), brings a rake of co
trucks down the rope-worked Wal
ridge Bank Incline at Stella Gill
County Durham. This was part of t
original Stanhope & Tyne Railw
through route of 1834, replaced by
deviaton through Beamish which
seen in *Plate 122*. It had a gradie
of about 1 in 24, and was the last of t
S&TR rope-worked inclines in us
closing in 1969. There was a lev
crossing across the incline, about o
third of the way up, and its gates ca
be seen closed across the line. It mu
have been tricky to work. The rop
itself can be seen lying on its rolle
between the rails, and was not hooke
on to the engine for the descent.

Plate 122: In 1919 Sir Vincent Raven brought out the final NER 0-8-0 design, his Class T3 (LNER Class Q7), with three cylinders instead of two. A member of this class is seen here banking an iron-ore train from Tyne Dock to Consett, just at the bottom of the 1 in 56 gradient from South Pelaw, on the deviation line which avoided the Waldridge and other inclines of the original Stanhope & Tyne Railway route. This original route appears in the foreground, and in *Plate 121*. Beside the tender is a tall NER slotted post home and distant signal. The large Westinghouse pump on the engine footplating is not original, but was fitted by BR to operate the doors of the iron-ore wagons.

Plate 123: The earlier-designed NER 0-8-0 engines were more numerous than the Class Q7, and had only two cylinders. They were LNER Class Q6 (NER Class T2). One of the later members of the class, No. 63418, drifts carefully down the 1 in 71 gradient from Consett Station (in the far distance) towards Consett East Junction where the connection to Blackhill and the Derwent Valley line branched off. The driver is obviously intent on keeping his long train well under control, as the branch turnout was very sharp.

Plate 124: Steam and electric trains shared the same tracks from South Shields to Tyne Dock, where we see the 5.40p.m. train to Sunderland in August 1956. As usual it is a three coach push-pull set, with Class G5 No. 67259 in charge, the leading carriage being a North Eastern eight compartment third. The general air of tidiness around stations was common in the North-East, and the station nameboard stands neatly in its own little patch, with whitewashed concrete edging around it. The edging, which appeared everywhere, was an innovation of John Miller, mentioned earlier.

Plate 125: There was an hourly regular interval service of steam trains between Sunderland and South Shields, and No. 67338 is seen propelling its push-pull set, chimney first, at Harton, on its way from South Shields to Sunderland. The coach next to the engine is another NER eight compartment third. The ballast looks dirty, but colliery subsidence in this area made maintenance a ganger's nightmare. The coal cage on the engine's bunker can be compared with the GCR variety seen in *Plate 67*.

Plate 126: One of the last Class J27 locomotives to remain in service was No. 65842, built in 1908 and seen here in the Team Valley. Its rugged simplicity is visually unchanged in any major way, after fifty years of banging about with North-eastern goods and mineral workings. The rope-worked Bowes Railway (NCB) passed underneath the East Coast Main Line near here. On this fine evening the crew have no need of their storm sheet, which is rolled up on the rear edge of the cab roof, as they drift back to the shed at the end of the day.

Plate 127:   The last duties for the Class D20 engines were with stopping trains, running the 34 miles north from Newcastle to Alnwick. In this view, No. 62383 calls at Manors, with the 5.04p.m. service from Newcastle on 14th August 1956, to pick up homegoing passengers from the north side of the city. In the distance the spire of St. Nicholas Cathedral puts in an appearance. The lines on the right of the picture lead to the triangle at South Gosforth, used mainly by the electric trains.

Plate 128:   Just as it must have been doing for over fifty years, Class J25 No. 65727 (NER Class P1) was working a loose-coupled mineral train in the summer of 1956. The scene is Newsham, south of Blyth, focus of the Blyth & Tyne coal traffic, and the train is leaving the line from Bedlington. The route to Blyth goes off to the right. Coal trains were as old as railways in this district, and some of the last steam workings in the North-East were in this Northumberland coalfield. The only new things were the post-war 'prefabs' seen on the left.

Plate 129: Class J26 and J27 locomotives were the successors to the Class J25s, and designated Classes P2 and P3 by the NER. For years their large boilers made them notable among 0-6-0 engines. No. 65810 from South Blyth Shed is seen at Newsham, on the Blyth & Tyne Railway, and the first four wagons of its train are of the NER 20 ton hopper type, although some of the ones in this 1956 picture look suspiciously new. Could it be that BR was actually building new examples as late as this? Note the short-armed signals, controlling movements on the goods line. The passenger lines are beyond.

Plate 130: The 1872 extension to Newbiggin-by-the-Sea was the last act of the Blyth & Tyne Railway's push northwards through the Northumberland Coalfield. By August 1956, the terminus looks rather forlorn in the rain as Class G5 No. 67341 waits with the 3.40p.m. service to Monkseaton. The vehicles in the bay are not through coaches from King's Cross to this remote seaside, but a pair of Gresley-designed parcels vans. The other stock is NER.

Plate 131: Alnmouth Shed was the home of the last survivors of Class D20 locomotives. In this picture, No. 62375, of 1906, is observed shunting around the station and yard at Alnwick, which could only be described as palatial. William Bell's handsome station of 1887, although typical of NER opulence, was something of an overprovision, but it must be remembered that the Duke of Northumberland lived nearby, and the Percy Lion on its monument is visible over the trees. Of railway interest are the loading gauge on the left, and an NER signal on a lattice post.

Chapter Five

The North British

My introduction to the East Coast railways in Scotland came in 1948. Travelling northwards by the 'Flying Scotsman', our journey had not been without incident. While lunching at Grantham, after a 10a.m. start, we were suddenly told to remove our luggage from our first class compartment 'because the carriage is on fire', although I expect it was just a hot box. My mother's annoyance at losing her reserved seat was relieved by being allowed to travel the remainder of the way to Edinburgh in the restaurant car. In fact, it was a Great Northern twelve wheeler and rather more comfortable than what we had abandoned, and the close-carpeted entrance vestibule was rather like the hall in our Edwardian house, and nearly as large. The incident at Grantham was compounded by other delays, and we ran into (Edinburgh) Waverley in the dark. I was 'all eyes' for my first sight of a North British engine, and was leaning out of the window. In the gloom we passed an engine on the next track and all I could tell of it was the end part of its name, '. . .ss' painted on a splasher. I thought it must be *Loch Ness*, and the fact that I could find no such engine in any list did not put me off. In fact it was a 'Glen', *Glen Luss*, but to me, my first Scottish engine was *Loch Ness*.

We stayed at the Caledonian Hotel, at the other end of Princes Street, and left for Glasgow the next day, so my acquaintance with Waverley was delayed until the following year. This time we stayed properly, at the North British Hotel. Using field glasses I could watch the engines far below at the west end of the station, and such was the post-war delapidation that I could see them through the holes in the station roof as well.

Time and the planners have not disturbed that powerful trinity of station, hotel and the Scott monument; they are as much Edinburgh as the Castle. When I started railway photography a few years later, I made my way to Waverley, but it is not an easy place to get good pictures. I have often wished that I had begun to use a camera earlier, but with

the NBR I was lucky because the slaughter of pre-grouping engines really began in the mid-1950s, after I had taken quite a lot of pictures. The earliest ones in this chapter were taken in 1951, but I soon transferred my attentions to Glasgow where there seemed to be more variety.

Glasgow (Queen Street) was worse than Waverley for photography but Cowlairs Incline was another matter, and there are two pictures of it here. One is of a Scottish 'Director' battling its way up the 1 in 42, while the other shows one of the Class N15 bankers manfully and noisily bringing up the rear of the cavalcade, the head of which is proclaimed by a plume of smoke on the horizon. The incline has long been an attraction for photographers, and my first knowledge of it came from one of Tice Budden's delightful pictures, dating from the time when cable assistance was still used.

In the 1950s, Queen Street (Low Level) was still entirely inhabited by steam trains, and it could be a fairly murky spot on a wet day. Virtually all trains were worked by Gresley 2-6-2 tanks, and when electric trains came I was glad I had condescended to take some pictures of them, as for me, at that time, the real interest in suburban trains lay in the occasional one that was not worked by a Class V1. By this time, I had kind and knowing friends in Glasgow who led me to the right places. In those days Glasgow men often came home from the city for lunch, the 1950s probably being the last decade with four rush hours a day on the trains. People still worked on Saturday mornings then too.

My visits to Scotland were often voyages of discovery, and on one of them I arrived in that treasure house of pre-grouping engines, the Kingdom of Fife. Reference books say that its capital is Cupar, but I know it is really Thornton Junction. From that unprepossessing spot, its wood and ash platforms heaving up and down because of the coal workings beneath, a series of lines radiated north, south, east and west. Each brought its quota of coal trains and empties, often worked by the Class J37 engines which were the NBR's ultimate goods locomotives. Indeed, they had been pitted against English eight-coupled types, and although they were outclassed they were not disgraced.

As well as this abundance of NBR goods engines, many of the passenger trains were worked by 'Glen' and 'Scott' class locomotives, lightly loaded but still earning their keep. Although rarely clean, their appearance had not been altered much by the LNER, and they retained a very real dignity in their declining years. In addition to the engines, Thornton had other attractions; it was such a friendly place. Authority did not frown on a wandering photographer, and I was even invited to shelter in the main signal box during a thunderstorm, to be entertained by those present with a series of anecdotes about their colleagues and their professional habits. Alas the Fifeshire accents were so strong that I missed the punchline of every single story but not so the assembled company, as the box rang with their laughter. Then the sun came out and they went back to work, so I went back to the photographic delights of Thornton Junction. It was an unforgettable place.

I hope no one will be disappointed by the scarcity of West Highland pictures in this chapter. To this day I haven't visited Mallaig, and have visited Fort William only once. The latter was by a 15/- Sunday excursion from Queen Street (Low Level), on a dull and rainy day. The train started, I believe, from Airdrie and, as it picked up at suburban stations along the north bank of the Clyde towards Dumbarton, the prospects were not good. Many fishermen joined us, encumbered with rods and bottles of cheap red wine with which they were already fortifying themselves. Suddenly, at Arrochar I think it was, they one and all alighted, and the long train was left to a few family parties on a day trip, and two railway enthusiasts. At Ardlui the sun came out, and the rest of the day was beautiful. Coming back we had a cheap and satisfying fish tea in the restaurant car, and I even managed a clandestine footplate ride on the Class K2. I don't remember seeing any other trains at all, so Lord's Day Observance must still have been a force to be acknowledged, and one West Highland tradition not honoured that day was seeing the 'Arrochar Motor'. This was a two or three coach push-pull set running between Craigendoran and Arrochar, and motive power was invariably one or other of the last remaining Class C15 4-4-2 tanks. They were kept clean, I think, by regular crews who cared for them.

The great gathering ground for the larger NBR 4-4-2 tanks was the Dundee & Arbroath Joint line. Their existence and activity came as a most gratifying surprise, like finding the Robinson 4-4-2 tanks so plentiful at Manchester (London Road). I suppose I should have known about these things from an intelligent inspection of the engine allocation lists, but somehow it never occurred to me to do this kind of research. To a degree, one relied on word of mouth reports from other people in search of pre-grouping material, but sometimes one just stumbled across an enclave of the system filled with desirable things, and that was always a marvellous moment. The Dundee & Arbroath Joint line seemed to have maintained a singular identity in many ways, because ten years after nationalisation many of its tickets were still of a Joint line printing, and some of them looked pre-grouping. The carriages were not; in fact, the mixed LMS/LNER look of them reminded me of the CLC. My day north of the Tay was well spent.

This chapter includes one picture that is not of a train, but which could not be left out. I was brought to the old NBR coach body at Burntisland by that same kind friend who had so often guided me towards unusual items in Glasgow. By now he had risen to the rank of stationmaster, and I was given the run of his territory. He was not, by the way, responsible for the disgraceful incident at Kirkaldy, when one of the Class J88 harbour shunters finished a journey down in the waters of the dock. The ancient appearance of these engines, which was contrived by a small boiler of low pitch surmounted by an exceedingly long and slender chimney, never failed to impress visitors from England. Some had stovepipe chimneys which looked even longer, and one still had the lock-up safety-valves in the dome. All had dumb buffers to add to the general air of antiquity which was totally misleading, because the oldest member of the class dated from 1904 and the youngest from 1919. The other surviving NBR 0-6-0 tank, the Class J83, was at least visually descended from Stroudley's 'Terrier' class, and although belonging to a previous generation, didn't look like it.

Another locomotive antiquity was the 'Wee Puggies', the 0-4-0 Class Y9 saddle tanks, the oldest of which was built in 1882. Dumb-buffered again and often stovepiped, they looked their age, but the thing which, to me, quite distinguished them was the ramshackle wooden tenders which many had for permanent companions. The appearance of these vehicles was somewhat equivocal, being half-way between a wagon and a coal cart - they carried no water - and although some were close-coupled to the engine, others were not. The ensemble reminded me of a respectable if impoverished citizen, accompanied by a disreputable and none too sober acquaintance, from whom he was trying in vain to keep his distance. Nevertheless they did many years of useful work round the sharp curves in the docks and factories of industrial Scotland, and I enjoyed their survival, and all my forays into North British Railway territory. Lovers of that railway will find more pictures of its engines in the chapter on the Great North of Scotland section, as some of its locomotives migrated there. It had quite a different, almost urbane atmosphere, while the NBR was rough-hewn, even craggy. Apart from the engines, the memory which abides is of a surpassing warmth and friendliness.

Plate 132: Lochgelly, on the Thornton to Cowdenbeath line, was in the middle of a coalfield, and the platforms suffered badly from mining subsidence, as the angle of the gaslamp testifies. In this wilderness the staff made a brave effort with flowering shrubs and plants, and the scene was deceptively rural. 'Scott' class No. **62436** *Lord Glenvarloch* is framed by the footbridge as it pauses with a local train in 1957, the bridge being of a pattern much used by the NBR.

Plate 133: Proudly pulling out of Waverley Station in 1952, is No. 62470 *Glen Roy*, a member of Class D34 (NBR Class K or 'Superheated Intermediate'), at the head of a slow train to the Kingdom of Fife. The Glens' were the last express passenger design of W. P. Reid for the NBR, and outlasted the more famous 'Scott' class, and the Atlantics. The leading brake is North British, as is the towering edifice of the hotel in the distance.

Plate 136 (below): A 'Scott' class 4-4-0 with an empty stock train, just west of the Mound Tunnel in Edinburgh. As well as the shed plate 62A, it still carries the shed name, Thornton, on the buffer beam, as in LNER days. The neo-classical portico of the Scottish National Gallery, built on the Mound, is just visible over the trees. On either side of the line are Princes Street Gardens, so this is no place to have a smoky fire.

Plate 134 (left upper): The west end shunter at Waverley, in September 1952, was this Class J83 tank, built for the NBR in 1901 as Class D. It is enjoying a brief respite from the constant activity of a passenger pilot at a busy station such as this, where there was an endless succession of vehicles to be attached and detached. The engine's next move will be to couple an eight-wheeled Pullman car, which can just be seen, to an outgoing train. It was built by Clayton Waggons Ltd., of Lincoln in 1923, and rejoiced in the name of *Mauchline Belle*, before being sold to the LMS in 1933, and ending its life prosaically numbered SC218M.

Plate 135 (left lower): A member of Class N15 (NBR Class A) on pilot duties at Edinburgh (St. Margaret's), in September 1951. Like many NBR tank engines, it had an extra handrail on the bunker side and the shunter's footboard below. The nearby handcrane was, I suspect, far older than the engine, and the whole complex at St. Margaret's, the original base for engineering operations on the NBR, was something of a working museum of antique railway plant.

Plate 137 (below):   As befitted an early trunk line, the earthworks of the Edinburgh & Glasgow Railway were on a grand scale, as we can see in this picture of Class J36 No. 65270 in the deep cutting near Bishopbriggs. However, the result of the earthworks was easy gradients, so this local goods can make good speed as it hurries to get clear of the main line at Cowlairs.

Plate 138 (right upper):   Just down the line from the point depicted in *Plate 137,* another '18 incher', No. 65295, plods along the Edinburgh & Glasgow Railway main line with a load of 35 wagons and a brake; a familiar lowland scene in 1957. The original classification of these engines was Class C, and this one served the NBR and its successors from 1897 until 1961.

Plate 139 (right lower):   LNER 'Director' class No. 62687 *Lord James of Douglas,* built by Armstrong Whitworth in 1924, heads an eight coach train of mainly Gresley stock up the Cowlairs Incline from Glasgow (Queen Street) on 1st August 1953. Compare the cut-down boiler mountings for the NBR section with those on the GCR's 'Director' class engines. These Northern Area engines, however, retained the wheel and handle fastening for the smokebox door, which their counterparts in England lost.

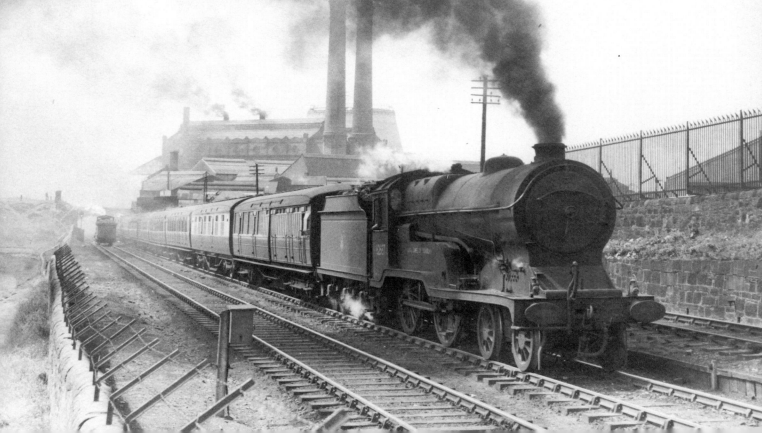

Plate 140: The other end of the train shown in *Plate 139*, with one of the faithful Class N15 bankers hard at work on the 1 in 42 gradient to Cowlairs. The noise was immense, but the locals were completely used to it and took no more notice of the trains than they did of the two trams in the Keppochill Road. The banking engine is fitted with a special slip coupling at the front, so that it can disengage from the train without the need for a stop at the top of the bank.

Plate 141: Saturday commuting Glasgow, illustrated by the 12.4 p.m. Springburn to Hyndland tra at Partick (NBR), renamed Partic Hill by April 1957. The engine Class J37 No. 64581. The ten ments here looked grimmer tha those around Cowlairs, but note th alarming condition of the chimne of the waiting-room on the f platform.

Plate 142: The train shown in *Plate 141* would have diverged from the line to Dumbarton, at Partick Hill Junction, and passed on to the short branch to the terminus at Hyndland. This is the interior of Partick Hill Junction signal box, in 1957, entirely traditional in its layout and equipment. I think the illuminated track circuit diagram above the block instrument shelf was the only major addition since North British Railway days.

Plate 143: A Clydebank workers' train approaching Whiteinch West Junction in 1959, with Class J37 No. 64639 and a Gresley two coach articulated set, leading the 5.22p.m. service from Clydebank (East) to Springburn. From the position of the signals in the background, the train appears to be routed via Maryhill and Cowlairs, rather than Queen Street (Low Level), but I cannot find any trace of it in the timetable. The line coming in from the left once gave access to the NBR's Whiteinch (Victoria Park) Station.

Plate 144:   On a misty April morning in 1957, Class N15 No. 69166 brings a train of empty cattle trucks round the curve from Whiteinch North Junction to Whiteinch East Junction. Jordanhill Station platform is on the extreme left. Compared with *Plate 143*, there are no signs of impending electrification.

Plate 145:   Sabbath calm at Eastfield Shed in 1953, with Class J88 (NBR Class F) No. 68327, dumb-buffered like all her clan, in company with a West Highland Class K2 and an NER tank No. 68733. The sun highlights a safety-valve trumpet, while a latter-day Buster Keaton uses a coupling rod for a lunchtime seat. Even at this, one of Scotland's largest sheds, there was nothing much happening on a Sunday.

Plate 146: The very first of the NBR 0-6-2 tanks, No. 69120 of 1909, in the carriage sidings at Cowlairs. This class had a long and arduous life, the last member of it not being scrapped until 1962. The vehicle next to the engine is an NBR six-wheeled van, by 1953 used to convey stores from Cowlairs Works to depots all over the region.

Plate 147: High tide at Craigendoran, with the 'Arrochar Motor' at the waterside on 26th August 1959. The lines on this side of the platform lead to Helensburgh, and the West Highland line is out of sight to the right, already at a higher level as it begins its climb into the mountains ahead.

Plate 148 (below): High above Gareloch, near Faslane, in the summer of 1959, the faithful 'Yorkie' heads the afternoon motor train from Arrochar to Craigendoran. The Class C15 engines (NBR Class M) were given their nickname because they were built by the Yorkshire Engine Co., of Sheffield, in 1911.

Plate 149 (right upper): Fort William's Sunday quiet is broken by the arrival of the Glasgow excursion, and as the passengers disperse to enjoy the sunlit waters of Loch Linnhe, Class J36 No. 65318 takes the stock away for cleaning. How we wished it could have done a quick run to Mallaig and back during the afternoon.

Plate 150 (right lower): The West Highland Railway was legally and financially an independent company until 1902, so one ponders over the legal force of a 'Warning to Trespassers pursuant to the NBR Act 1894' as exhibited at Fort William. Maybe it was ignored!

Plate 151 (left upper): The curving platforms at Inverkeithing, such a hindrance to starting a heavy south-bound train, provide the setting for No. 62478 *Glen Quoich*, which has just arrived with the 3.50p.m. from Dunfermline. This part of Scotland abounded in short workings of this type, all fitting into a local pattern of need, and many converging on Inverkeithing, the key to the Forth Bridge giving access to all the NBR lines south of the Firth of Forth, which divided the company's system into two halves.

Plate 152 (left lower): Heavy trains going south were often banked from Inverkeithing up the 1 in 70 incline to the Forth Bridge, and Class J35 No. 64480 (NBR Class B) was on this duty on 22nd April 1957. The splitting distants are for Inverkeithing Central Junction, where the lines to Dunfermline and Burntisland diverged, going west and east respectively, along the north side of the Firth of Forth.

Plate 153 (above): The 12.48p.m. service from Crail completes it runs along the north shore of the Firth of Forth, arriving at Thornton Junction behind the first 'Glen', No. 62467 *Glenfinnan*. *Plate 157* gives a closer view of the junction with the East of Fife line. By the late 1950s, the 'Glens' and 'Scotts' were used indiscriminately by sheds possessing both classes, although only the former, with 6ft. wheels, were strictly 'mixed traffic'.

Plate 154 (below): A proud portrait of No. 62441 *Black Duncan* at Dunfermline in 1957. Although only booked for a local working, the locomotive's powerful good looks suggest it would be ready to take on any passenger train in Scotland. Whoever picked the names for the 'Scott' class made a good choice with this one.

Plate 155: Dunfermline's 'Pug' and its disreputable companion in 1958. The Class Y9 engine sports a particularly forbidding stove-pipe chimney, as well as the usual extension tubes over the safety-valves. It was the only member of the class to have the vacuum brake, for carriage shunting at Dunfermline where this picture was taken. The NBR class nomenclature was G.

Plate 156: The final development of NBR goods power was the massive Class J37 0-6-0, (NBR Class B). Here, No. 64616 pulls away from Thornton Junction with a heavy train in September 1959. Its boiler still has the NBR pattern of lock-up safety-valves, rather than the newer 'pop' variety. The engine was built by the North British Locomotive Co., at the Atlas Works, Glasgow, in 1920, and was scrapped in 1963.

te 157: In this view of the junction
h the East of Fife line at the north
d of Thornton Junction Station, the
nalling is almost as interesting
the train. Most prominent are the
y pair of upper quadrant signals,
ornton Junction Station home and
ornton Junction Central distant.
ey control the East Coast Main Line,
d their height gives drivers coming
th a long distance view of the state
the junction. Beneath them is a
bby 'calling-on' arm, and to the left
signals controlling entry to subsidi-
lines. Next on the right is an upper
drant which is 'off' for the train,
12.08p.m. to Crail. Immediately
ow it we can just see Thornton
iction North signal box. The East of
e line goes off to the right to Leven,
Cameron Bridge, with lower quad-
t signals in the far distance 'off'
this train. Lastly, seen above the
liery tip heap, are the NBR pattern
er quadrants, by Stevens & Co.,
ich correspond to the upper quad-
ts guarding the line from Thornton
rth. Behind the train, which is
ded by No. 62418 *The Pirate,* is
ornton Junction Station signal box.

Plate 158: A glance at a map shows that Alloa was at the western end of the North British Railway territory north of the Firth of Forth, with only Stirling and the long-closed line towards the Trossachs and Balloch beyond it. The NBR had a small stone shed there, and in March 1959 one of the massive Class J37 goods engines was simmering outside it in the sunshine. The modest office accommodation on the right is a pair of North British third class coaches of the 1870s.

Plate 161 (right upper): A Class J3 No. 64549, heads a short goods train of mainly empty coal wagons, away from Thornton Junction towards Cardenden on 16th September 1959. By this time the 'Glen' and 'Scott' class locomotives were nearly all gone, with diesel multiple units having taken their place.

Plate 162 (right lower): Pictured leaving Dunfermline (Upper), is the 4.0 p.m. service to Thornton Junction. This was the return working of the train shown in *Plate 160*, seen here behind a 'Scott' class 4-4-0. As the background reminds us, goods and mineral traffic was more important to the railways than passengers in this part of Scotland.

Plate 159 (above): First class North British Railway accommodation of 1869, grounded at Burntisland 92 years later, can be compared with the coaches seen in *Plate 158*. Time and the weather have revealed ghostly traces of the NBR lettering.

Plate 160 (below): Thornton Junction Station's platforms were made of ashes and timber, as witness to mining subsidence in the heart of the Fifeshire Coalfield. As well as No. 62436 *Lord Glenvarloch*, waiting to leave with the 1.52p.m. working to Dunfermline (Upper) on 22nd April 1957, the scene includes a Caledonian intruder. It is No. 55217, an 0-4-4 tank. The 'rustic' platform seats, made from cast iron, were particularly incongrous in this industrial location.

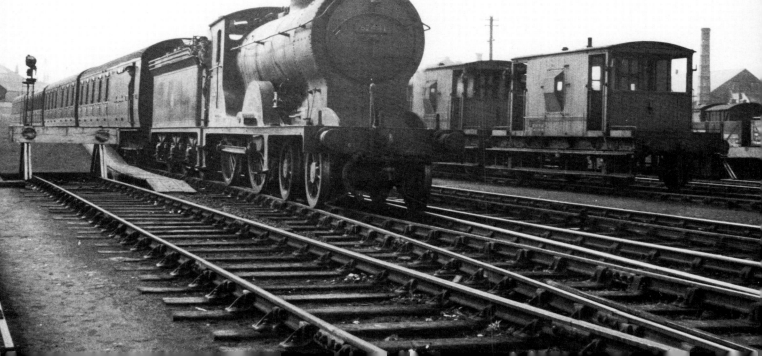

Plate 163 (above): Trains on the Dundee & Arbroath Joint Line used Dundee (East) Station, via Camperdown East Junction, rather than Dundee (Tay Bridge) which was the North British station. The end of the platform of West Ferry Station, the last before Dundee, can just be seen in this picture of the 1.09p.m. Saturday semi-fast train from Arbroath on 5th April 1958. The engine is Class C16 No. 67486 (NBR Class L), with the usual four coach Joint line formation.

Plate 164 (below): The last Class C16 locomotive, No. 67502 of 1921, nears Arbroath with a train from Dundee. Unlike the Class C15, they were built at the Atlas Works of the North British Locomotive Co. The coaches of this train, like most other Joint line services are a mixture of LMS (leading) and LNER stock. The stone boundary wall must make a good windbreak when the wind blows from the Tay Estuary in the background, but it was too early in the year for lingering on park seats, as the naked branches of the trees indicate. These stone boundary walls were quite a feature of the Joint line.

Plate 165 (right upper): Arbroath's ? lit station provides the setting for this ? of a Class C16 on a Dundee & Arbr? Joint line working. Steam from the W? inghouse pump indicates that air bra? was still in use on the engine in 1? although not on the train itself, and picture illustrates well the smoke? wingplates which these engines retai? unlike the 4-4-0s. The station nameb? is in the Scottish Region pale blue white style.

Plate 166 (right lower): Waiting for road, at the west end of Arbroath Stat? the train shown in Plate 165, heade? No. 67486, catches the spring sunsh? Notice the extensive use of the local st? for building, as well as for walls, a? Plate 164.

Plate 167: Long ago, the NBR ha been treated by the Caledonian Rai way as a gross intruder at Aberdee but by April 1954, that was all in th past and Class D34 No. 62482 *Gle Mamie* was allocated to the GNS shed at Kittybrewster. Here, betwee Aberdeen and Ferryhill, the locom tive waits, with a long Great North Scotland Section goods train, for road north through the Joint station.

Plate 168:   No. 67501 was a Class C16 engine allocated to Aberdeen, and is shown here making a spirited start from the south end of the station. Alas, all this show of effort was only for a shunt move, though the vehicles being shunted were for the famous 'West Coast Postal', the 3.30p.m. from Aberdeen.

The title of this chapter chose itself, although the fact is that long ago the Great North of Scotland had been a really awful railway. One of my regrets is that I was so keen to get out and about on the main line, that I never spared the time for a few minutes walk along the quays of Aberdeen to see the original terminus. Its shabby and cavernous depths were supposed to be a good indication of what the GNSR was like in the bad old days. There was a time when I set out to travel every mile of the GNSR, but the branch to the old station on the quay was one I missed.

Although my first meeting with the GNSR was when I saw one of its engines go by, while our car was stopped at a level crossing somewhere in the wilds, I really first came to know it at Aberdeen, this being usual for Southerners. In fact, it was on a day trip from Glasgow that started in the small hours. The day ticket only took you to Stirling, so there was a hectic dash out to the booking office there to buy another day ticket to Aberdeen, and you had to be in the right place in the train to do it in time. Railway staff were supposed to stop this sort of thing, 'rebooking by the same train', but they didn't seem to bother with us. In succeeding years I made a base at Aberdeen, and set out daily from there to explore the North-East of Scotland.

There were only two trains on which to travel, these being the through train to Inverness, which would take you to Keith and the west, and the other going due north for Fraserburgh and Peterhead on the Buchan line. An early start, with porridge compulsory, was called for, and it was necessary to plan any expedition with some care because there weren't many trains. Often a branch would be explored by doubling back from station to station, getting a picture at each of them with the train either arriving or leaving. Sometimes the timetable just wouldn't fit, and there was nothing for it but to walk from one station to the next.

The two groups of lines leading from the parting of the ways at Dyce had quite different atmospheres. One was obviously the main line, but the eastern lines had no such feeling and everybody there appeared more relaxed. I had the first of many footplate trips on a Class D40, between Peterhead and Maud, and took the inevitable spectacle-glass view. It was a picture just begging to be taken, compelling by the shapeliness of the curves along the boiler top. On that same trip I was treated to a close up of the simple but effective Manson tablet exchanger in action, as seen from the footplate.

In those days it was not oil but cattle which was the main source of prosperity in this eastern part of the GNSR territory, and special trains were often run in connection with the markets held each week. Maud Junction was quite a local centre of this activity, and when I arrived there from Peterhead, one market day, the station was crowded. There was a refreshment room on the island platform, housed in a low stone building and run by private enterprise. Foraging for some lunch, I went in the door or, rather, I tried to go in the door but met a wall of bodies. The room was packed solid with farmers and dealers, with one and all discussing 'the price o' beasts'. When I did manage to push my way through this throng to the counter, the only solid nourishment on sale was hot roast beef sandwiches. In that company they would not have dared to serve up anything but the best, and I don't think I have yet tasted finer beef. It really was a case of living off the country.

The lines to Fraserburgh and Peterhead were, like most of the GNSR, single with passing places. The Peterhead branch seemed subsidiary to the other, although the timetable indicated differently. The trains split and joined at Maud Junction, so several times a day there was a lot of

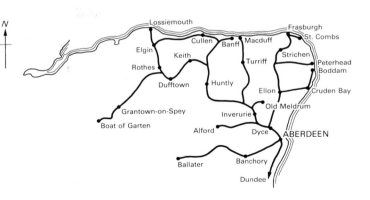

movement back and forth, so much so that, contrary to what one might expect, the 'up' and 'down' services between Aberdeen and the coast didn't cross there. With all the necessary shunting, there just was not room. I don't want to give the impression of Maud being comparable to Clapham Junction, as the whole Buchan line's passenger service could be accommodated on one small timetable page, with connections far and wide thrown in for good measure. I don't think they had too much trouble finding room for the cattle trains on market days. Before I leave this section of the GNSR, I must mention the Fraserburgh & St. Combs Light Railway. It ran twice as many trains each day as the line connecting Fraserburgh with Aberdeen, and yet it had more of a true light railway character than any other I know. As it threaded through what in Scotland is called the 'Links', the line formation followed closely the lie of the ground. The track was laid rather like a by-road; there seemed to be no fences, and people wandered about across it as if it was a cart track and not a railway at all.

The main line northwards from Dyce was altogether a more formal affair, as befitted a route on which ran through trains to Inverness, one with a restaurant car which, in GNSR days, was hired from the NBR. The crew of that car worked a long day, starting with late breakfasts just after 8a.m. and finishing with early high teas on the run into Aberdeen around 5p.m. The principal trains on the main line usually split into three portions along the way, with the first split coming at the isolated exchange platform at Cairnie Junction, where a section was detached for 'Elgin via the Coast'. The next came at Keith Junction where the remainder of the train divided, with both halves going on to Elgin, one by the Highland route (the Mulben line) and the other by the GNSR route via Craigellachie. The latter, although longer and slower than the Highland route, was a nicer ride but, more importantly, it gave a connection at Craigellachie on to the beautiful Speyside line.

This was a real backwater, with Grantown-on-Spey being the only place of any size. The branch ended at the Highland Railway station at Boat of Garten. It was here, I believe, that the GNSR once tried to seduce southbound passengers off Highland trains, with the pleasures of getting to England by way of Aberdeen and the East Coast route. In BR days, the sign merely said 'change for Speyside line'. If the latter was still open today, all the way past so many distilleries, I suppose they would run whisky tasting excursions, but in the 1950s it was only a very lovely branch. One of two carriages used was often a GNSR six compartment corridor composite and, being an Edwardian vehicle, it was a great novelty to me because of the doors between compartment and corridor. Having been brought up in the south, where these were of the sliding variety, I knew no others. But in this glorious GNSR carriage, these were proper doors which opened out into the corridor. They have preserved a Class D40 locomotive, and I hope they have kept one of the carriages too.

On one visit to Strathspey we were caught in a real summer downpour, and got thoroughly soaked while walking back from Aberlour to Craigellachie. Such is the nature of a Highland rainstorm that the sun had come out by the time we arrived at Elgin, on our way to visit the Lossiemouth line. The crew of the branch engine took pity on our bedraggled appearance, and we were invited to 'dry your breeks by the fire' on the Class D40. We were still on the footplate, our trousers steaming gently, when the train set off for Lossiemouth, so we had a ride on the engine for good measure. I reflected how the young Ramsay MacDonald, who was born in 'Lossie', might well have dried out like us by the fire of the branch engine in the 1880s, probably one of the old 2-4-0s. He certainly rode on them.

In the 1950s there were three substantial branches of the GNSR which had no passenger trains. By permission, I managed to travel over two of them, the Alford and the Banff, Macduff & Turriff branches. The former left the main line at Kintore, near Inverurie, and the engine was an NBR Class J36 0-6-0. After the soaking of the previous day, we enjoyed some dry weather, and spent a rather remote morning going gently up to Alford. Vandalism had not yet appeared in the land and the station there was in good order, with even the clock still going. Like the North Eastern Railway, the GNSR sometimes incorporated clocks into the fabric of the building, with the works inside and a face showing on to the platform. There was a turntable at Alford and so the engine was duly turned, and we regained the main line about lunchtime with another branch 'in the bag'.

After many weary years of trying to look after its engines at Kittybrewster, the early years of this century saw the prospering GNSR open a new locomotive and carriage works at Inverurie, 16 miles out on the main line. It was well and almost lavishly laid out, and served its first and subsequent owners very well for 60 years. While there were not many engines there at any one time, like most locomotive works, it had one never-failing source of interest; the scrap line. Here, after the visit to Alford, I found the last two Class D41 4-4-0s, one already being dismembered. I wish I had bought one of those beautiful chimneys. For good measure, a Caledonian 0-4-4 tank was also being cut

up because Inverurie, in BR ownership, had dealings with ex-LMS engines as well as the NBR and GNSR.

The other goods only line which appears in this chapter was the 30 mile Banff, Macduff & Turriff branch. By spending a night in Macduff we were able to catch the train when it set out for Inveramsey, early the next morning. Motive power was an NBR 'Glen' class and we had a fair load, although most stations were passed without stopping. There was, however, extensive shunting at Auchterless, where a large sign outside the station, in Scottish Region blue and white, announced 'AUCHTERLESS STATION AND POST OFFICE' despite being in the middle of nowhere. While I was chatting to the railwayman who did solitary duty there, he opened the drawer of a large desk, in the middle of his office, to reveal a jumble of pre-grouping timetables which had been there since the 1890s. Just as he invited me to help myself, the guard called out that we were going NOW, and I only had time to grab a handful and run. I've often wondered what became of that Aladdin's cave.

I suppose the 1950s was the last decade when there was always a sporting chance of picking up pre-grouping relics just for the asking. On one occasion, my parents wanted to see the Royal Family arrive at Ballater for their annual Balmoral holiday, so we drove over early one morning from Aberdeen to get a good view in the station square. After the excitement was over, and the crowds had dispersed, my mother decided she must have a cup of tea, so we adjourned to the station refreshment room. As we sat at our table, I was amazed to see that most of the crockery was GNSR. Only one thing prevented my pocketing a piece, the fact that every other table in the room was occupied by four policemen. Theft being impossible, I got a lesson in morality by being given some pieces just by asking the Manageress.

The Great North of Scotland system, although small, was compact, and had the air of being well run. I think that was partly due to the way the company had provided itself with durable buildings and equipment in its prosperous years, and as the picture of Alford shows even a quiet branch terminus was well and neatly made. A particular speciality I have seen nowhere else was the inscribing of the station name in gold-leaf block letters on the glass fanlight of the door from the platform to the booking hall. The large stations also benefited from GNSR spending, disagreeing with a GNR Chairman, who once ruefully remarked 'there is no money in stations'. That GNSR engines and carriages remained into BR days is not surprising because they were well made and, although non-standard, could be kept quite easily to their home system with Inverurie Works to look after them. Their survival added to the attractions of a part of Scotland rather off the tourist track; and who could forget that other GNSR August speciality of wild raspberries along the lineside, waiting for a passing photographer.

Plate 169: No. 62277 *Gordon Highlander* at Boat of Garten (Highland Railway) with the 10.18a.m. working from Craigellachie. Among the interesting features were the fine lamps, and the GNSR platform seat, the Highland two-wheeled luggage barrows and the fact that everyone in sight, in August 1953, is wearing a hat. On the far platform is a large blackboard on which the staff chalked up details of the timekeeping, or lack of it, of main line trains between Perth and Inverness.

Plate 170: A Great North of Scotland classic. Class D40 No. 62270 was the last of the unsuperheated 4-4-0s, built in 1915 to a design of 1899. It could trace its lineage back to the 1860s when the company had first made the 4-4-0 its standard wheel arrangement. A month after this picture was taken, at Peterhead on 5th August 1953, the engine was scrapped.

Plate 171: As well as the 4-4-0s, BR inherited four 0-4-2 tanks from the GNSR. Built in 1915 for working in the docks at Aberdeen, they retained their Manning Wardle details to the end, as well as some local peculiarities like the lamp irons, which were designed for the GNSR pattern lamps, with brackets on the side. No. 68190 is on the turntable at Kittybrewster in August 1953, while the carriage (SC19955M) to the left of the picture is possibly Caledonian.

Plate 172: Some GER Class B12s sent to the GNSR, still carried the small Belpaire boilers. In their new home they were so well-liked that some managed to get into the apple green livery after the war, which lasted into BR days. In this picture, a gleaming No. 61543 stands at the north end of Aberdeen Joint Station in September 1952, ready to leave on a Buchan line train.

Plate 173 (right upper): The island platform at Maud Junction, with No. 62276 *Andrew Bain* waiting to leave for Peterhead. On the left is the famous refreshment room, and in the goods yard on the right they are loading a cattle train. On the buffer-beam the shed allocation is still in the old style of K BREWSTER.

Plate 174 (right lower): Class B12 No. 61502 waits at Maud Junction for loading of its cattle special to be completed, before setting off for Aberdeen and the south in the summer of 1953. It is a long way from Liverpool Street, but at least it is heading in the right direction.

Plate 175: The 12.38p.m. working from Peterhead arrives at Maud Junction on 11th August 1954. The engine is No. 62278 *Hatton Castle,* with a GNSR carriage in BR red and white livery leading an NBR brake. The Fraserburgh line signals are on the left. All the named members of Class D40 were superheated, and were built 1920/21.

Plate 176: A picture taken on the Peterhead line, near Inverurie, from the footplate of Class D40 No. 62270, which was GNSR Class V, and built at Inverurie Works. The train was the 3.08p.m. from Peterhead, one of only two per day which stopped at Newseat Halt, located just around the corner ahead.

Plate 177: A typical view, from the carriage window, of the ups and downs of the St. Combs Light Railway, threading its way through the 'Links' beside the sea. By the time this picture was taken in 1954, motive power was an LMS type 2-6-0, but in earlier days this line had seen more exotic locomotives.

Plate 178: A former GER 1500 class (B12) leaves Keith Junction with the 12.20p.m. Keith Town to Aberdeen stopping train on 4th August 1953. The stock is all LNER, with an eight compartment third leading a pair of corridor coaches in the BR red and cream colours. Notice the crude way the LNER fitted the vacuum ejector pipe along the boiler, from the firebox shoulder to the smokebox, compared with the GER attention to the appearance of detail, as exemplified by the way the delivery pipe to the clack-box is exactly straight and vertical, and doubles as a handrail above the leading footsteps, themselves integral with the footplate valancing.

Plate 179: Just round the corner from the viewpoint in *Plate 178* was a stone-built engine shed. Inside were two Class D40s; No. 62273 *George Davidson*, under repair, and No. 62274 *Benachie*, which was in steam. *George Davidson* has its pistons and valves out, and the buffers are decorated with piston rings. Aside from its glories, the age of steam entailed generations of men looking after engines in ill-lit, dirty conditions like this, with precious little proper equipment to do it with. Yet they were dedicated, and proud of their calling.

Plate 180: The Speyside goods tra arrives at Keith Junction in 195 headed by the now-preserved N 62277 *Gordon Highlander*, which w once GNSR Class F. It had come fro Craigellachie as part of a regular wor ing, which operated when there w traffic for the direction of Aberdeen.

Plate 181: Summer sunshine at Craigellachie highlights Class D40 No. 62271 as it shunts the goods from the Speyside line, the train consisting mainly of cattle trucks. In the foreground is the back of a ground signal by Stevens & Co., who supplied the GNSR. A front view of one of these can be seen at Alford in *Plate 185*, and on the NBR in *Plate 157*. The line to Elgin is out of sight to the right, the single Speyside platform being one side of a 'V'- shaped station.

Plate 182: The wayside station at Aberlour in the rain, including a Class D40 locomotive at the platform with the train from Boat of Garten to Craigellachie. The branch had a modest three trains each way daily, and Advie Station only received one call in each direction, so it must have been a quiet spot.

Plate 185 (above): The closed passenger station at Alford in 1954, where No. 65213 is seen running round the goods. In the foreground is a front view of a Stevens ground signal (see Plate 181) in the 'off' position. Note the typical position of the clock and the station name, gold-lettered, on the fanlight over the main door from the platform. Goods traffic continued for some years after the passenger trains were taken off, as the new concrete storehouses show.

Plate 186 (below): Inverurie 'graveyard' in late 1953, with two of the last Class D41 engines waiting for the end. No. 62242 was built in 1895, while scrapping has already begun on a sister engine, No. 62231. Both had been GNSR Class T. A comparison of the shelter given by their cabs, when compared with those on the later D40 class, shows that life must have been hard in the winters before the newer engines appeared.

Plate 183 (left upper): A pleasing NSR ensemble in the bay platform at Elgin, where No. 62265 heads the p.m. train for Lossiemouth. The leading coach is a six compartment GNSR lavatory composite of about 1912 and, on the extreme left, are some grounded bodies from an earlier era, which seem to date from the bad old days of the 1860s. Similar vehicles took part in the Stockton & Darlington Centenary celebrations in 1925, and they were sold to the South Shields, Marsden & Whitburn Colliery Railway for their passenger usage.

Plate 184 (left lower): Monymusk station, on the Alford branch, with the daily goods headed by a North British Railway Class J36, No. 65213, on 12th August 1954. The passenger service had been withdrawn five years previously but everything is still in good order, even if the traffic is mainly ropes! This had been another GNSR branch with the three trains minimum service, this taking 36 minutes for the 5¾ miles, with four stops.

Plate 187: Further along the scrapping line, one of the early Class D40s is waiting to be cut up, after a collision with No. 62273 earlier in the year at Keith Shed. Behind is the remains of No. 55172, a Caledonian 0-4-4 tank.

Plate 188: Until 1951, when their trains were withdrawn, passengers on the erstwhile Banff, Macduff & Turriff Extension Railway must have been glad of the all-over roof of Macduff Station, perched on a windswept height above the town. On a gloomy August day in 1954, the goods train is ready to leave for Kittybrewster, behind 'Glen' class No. 62493 *Glen Gloy*. The signal is Stevens' pattern for the GNSR.

Plate 189:   The branch goods train at Turriff. Also featured is a typical GNSR signal box, rather curiously standing on piers well back from the platform. Access to it is by a palisaded catwalk. Note the stone faces of the platforms, and a rather openwork footbridge, common on the GNSR.

Plate 190:   Shunting at Auchterless, on the Macduff line, amid the rolling hills of Aberdeenshire. In 1954 there was still a useful amount of traffic, at least at some of the stations on the branch. The station and post office are just to the right of the single tree.

Tailpiece

Plate 191: Were ex-LNER engines regarded as intruders on former LMS lines, after the creation of British Railways? This NBR 0-6-0, Class J37 No. 64573, is seen working a coal train over the Glasgow & Paisley Joint line at Ibrox, while still shedded at Parkhead NBR. The North British Railway had running powers over the Joint line, which those deadly enemies the Caledonian and the Glasgow & South Western Railway had once worked in suspicious harness, so this 1959 intrusion, if such it was, had a long history. As it heads into the westering sun, the massive front end construction of the engine is apparent, as is the evidence on the lower part of the smokebox door of some extra heavy work quite recently.